PRAISE F(
THE HEALING POWE

"Dr. Rifkin's groundbreaking book gu ____ pathway to emotional health. His orig ____ ..._gci s power to energize the healing process provide a way to improve the efficiency and effectiveness of psychotherapy. When anger is bent into destructiveness, he shows how to unbend it into mental health. Every patient, person considering therapy or therapist can benefit from his clarity, insights and clear steps to emotional health."
— Ivan J. Miller, Ph.D., President of the Boulder Psychotherapists Guild and the Chair of the Board of the Colorado Patient Advocates, author of *What Managed Care Is Doing to Outpatient Mental Health: A Look Behind the Veil of Secrecy*

"John Rifkin, a gifted psychotherapist, tells us how we can lead happier lives not by stifling our anger but rather by using it constructively. In his straightforward, down-to-earth style, he shares with us easy-to-learn techniques for achieving greater emotional well-being."
— Evelyn Bassoff, Ph.D., author of *Mothers and Daughters: Loving and Letting Go*

"Drawing on 29 years of clinical experience, John Rifkin explains the multifaceted role of anger in a number of different life problems, ranging from difficulties in emotional intimacy to post-traumatic stress disorder, mood disorder, and addictions. He explains in a logical, understandable way how anger develops, what childhood experiences play a role in creating it, and, most importantly, how to go through the healing process inside and outside of psychotherapy. His approach is both insight- and skill-based. The reader will find his case studies illustrative and useful."
— David J. Miklowitz, Ph.D., author of *The Bipolar Survival Guide: What You and Your Family Need to Know*

"This excellent book is full of pearls and good advice for people with common psychological problems. Dr. Rifkin's extensive experience and wisdom shine through these pages, which are easily accessible to anyone who wishes a little more information and help coping with the miseries that afflict so many of us."
— Steven L. Dubovsky, M.D., Professor and Chair, Department of Psychiatry, University at Buffalo, Clinical Professor of Psychiatry and Medicine, University of Colorado

"Dr. Rifkin has crafted a profound yet easy-to-understand roadmap of the key emotions that drive our lives. This book is a 'must-read' for people trapped in the whirlpool of anger, sadness, or fear. The take-home value is immediate."
— Jim Warner, author of *Aspirations of Greatness: Mapping the Midlife Leader's Reconnection to Self and Soul*

# The Healing Power of Anger

## THE UNEXPECTED PATH TO LOVE AND FULFILLMENT

John R. Rifkin, Ph.D.

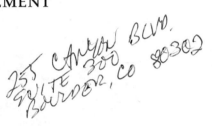

255 Canyon Blvd.
Suite 300
Boulder, CO 80302

Ron —
Here it is!
Hope you like it.
Let me know —
Best Wishes!
John

PARAVIEW
*Special Editions*

New York

Cover photo by Ariel Rifkin

ISBN: 1-931044-82-1

Library of Congress Control Number: 2004112534

The use of the love song poem from *Songmaster*, ©1978, is used with the kind
permission of Orson Scott Card.

The use of "Fear is the mind-killer" from *Dune*, by Frank Herbert, is used with
the kind permission of Matt Bialer, from the Trident Media Group, on behalf of
The Herbert Limited Partnership.

The use of the concept of the "therapeutic window" is used with the kind
permission of John Briere, Ph.D.

# CONTENTS

Introduction:    The Third Gift / 7

Chapter One:    Why Is There a Hole in Your Heart? / 13
                *The Source of Anger*

Chapter Two:    How to Unbend Your Anger / 27
                *Stop, Drop, and Roll*

Chapter Three:  The Bad Parent, "Good" Kid, and
                "Bad" Kid / 55
                *The Making of the Hole in Your Heart*

Chapter Four:   Anger and Anxiety / 85
                *"Fear Is the Mind Killer"*

Chapter Five:   Anger and Mood Disorders / 101
                *Depression Is a Parasite*

Chapter Six:    Anger and Addictions / 127
                *"Please Love Me!"*

Chapter Seven:  Anger and Intimacy / 153
                *"We Still Need the Eggs!"*

Chapter Eight:  How Do You Heal the Hole in Your Heart? / 179
                *"All You Need Is Love!"*

Chapter Nine:   Doing Whatever It Takes / 195

Acknowledgments

*This book is dedicated with love and appreciation
to my wife, Pamela Dee Rifkin.*

*"You are the flower of my winter;
you are the flower of my heart."*

# The Third Gift

*"Life is the first gift, love is the second
and understanding the third"*—MARGE PIERCY

ALMOST EVERYONE UNDERSTANDS ANGER'S POWER TO be destructive. People say things in anger that hurt other people's feelings. They can even act out their anger violently, causing physical injury and pain.

What is not well understood is that anger is a valuable part of the human emotional experience. Anger is not some dysfunctional, testosterone-induced malfunction in the human design. It is there for a reason and it is extremely valuable. *Your anger has the power to help you to heal the injuries both from your childhood as well as those that you currently experience in your daily life.* Anger is the natural healing energy that the body generates in response to injury. Along with sadness and fear, it is a secondary emotion that occurs in response to injury.

These ideas are the basis for this book, which is a tool that is meant to help you to harness the healing power of anger. As you read through the chapters, you will begin to understand the full meaning of anger and the role it is meant to play in the development of your own personal power and healing. You will also understand the role anger plays in many of the various problems in mental health, such as anxiety, mood disorders, and addiction. It will help you as you learn how to resolve conflicts in your intimate relationships so that they become healthier and more successful. You will also begin to understand the process of psychotherapy, both short and long term.

This book is the culmination of my twenty-eight years of experience in practicing psychotherapy. During my time in practice I have helped a lot of people and I've also learned a lot about the process of helping people. This book represents my desire to leave behind this gathering of knowledge and wisdom in order to help more people.

It was back in graduate school that I first thought I should write a book about anger. This was a time when no one had written much of anything on the subject. But life seemed to keep getting in the way—the business of marriage and fatherhood, as well as the business of building a successful practice. However, in the last few years I've taken the time to focus on this topic and this book. Perhaps that has something to do with my getting older.

After I had been in practice for only a few of my twenty-eight years, I wrote out a simple diagram. It was a representation of the triangular relationship of the Bad Parent, the "Good" Kid, and the "Bad" Kid which now appears in Chapter Three. It portrays the way a Bad Parent message causes an internal split in the child and begins the ongoing pattern of dysfunctional anger. It was a dynamic and a concept that occurred to me organically as I was working with people. I copied it so that I could hand it out to the clients with whom I worked.

Years later, I was asked by a psychiatrist colleague and friend, Richard Suddath, M.D., to run an in-patient group on anger for the mood disorders unit at Centennial Peaks Hospital in Louisville, Colorado. The administrative staff asked me to write a short statement for patients about anger and its relationship to depression and bipolar disorder. From that start, over the years the manuscript has grown and turned into this book, which I continue to give as a gift to clients when I begin working with them.

Throughout *The Healing Power of Anger: The Unexpected Path to Love and Fulfillment*, I use anecdotes. I do this for two reasons. One is that it is helpful to see how concepts work when real people use them. The other reason is that concepts, by themselves, are often boring. Seeing what people actually do with concepts is much more entertaining, as well as educational. None of the anecdotes in this book represents the real people I have worked with. I have gathered them from my clinical experience and changed the characters and circumstances significantly to protect the identity of my clientele. At the same time, the anecdotes will help you to understand your own psychological processes. By this I mean how you have been shaped emotionally by your childhood experiences and how these experiences continue to influence your behavior today, sometimes in unhealthy ways.

In addition, this book will help you to understand the difference between short- and long-term psychotherapy, what the goals of each are, and how to accomplish those goals. In terms of short-term work, you will learn a three-step system that is my version of cognitive behavioral therapy. It is different from most cognitive therapies in that it validates and includes emotions, and, what's more, actively uses them. I call this system *Stop, Drop, and Roll* because it's what you must do to put out the fire of dysfunctional uses of anger. It can help you reduce the symptoms of all emotional problems, as well as the problematic behaviors that can go with them.

Besides learning more about anger, you will learn what emotional intimacy is and what true love is all about. When applied to conflict resolution in relationships, Stop, Drop, and Roll—the same three steps used to put out angry fires—can help to reduce communication difficulties dramatically. You will also gain insight into how our families of origin impact our intimate relationships. You will also learn some techniques for reducing the distortions to communication caused by these early injuries. You will understand the difference between aggressive, passive-aggressive, and assertive behaviors.

Finally, I hope that you will be inspired to find the courage you need to make your life more fulfilled. Psychotherapy is hard work, whether that means merely fine tuning your life or fully healing the hole in your heart.

Before you dive into this book, I'd like to present an overview of the individual chapters.

Chapter One looks at how we develop the hole in our hearts, which is how I describe the basic injuries that can impact our lives in negative ways. This chapter will give you a greater understanding of the roles that anger, power, and intimacy play in life and injury.

Chapter Two will give you a full understanding of Stop, Drop, and Roll, the three-step system for dealing with problematic thoughts, feelings, and/or behaviors. It is an easy-to-understand, yet difficult-to-accomplish system that can turn around almost every dysfunctional situation related to anger.

Chapter Three explains how the hole in your heart was created. It defines and explains Bad Parenting. It also gives insight into the internal dynamics of the human psyche, in particular what I call the "Good" Kid and "Bad" Kid. In this chapter I also lay out my framework for diagnosing the seven categories of emotional damage in a family.

Chapter Four examines anxiety. It also explains why I have come to believe that Post-Traumatic Stress Disorder (PTSD) is the universal underlying diagnosis for all of us. In this chapter I also discuss the process of working to heal trauma, how to deal effectively with anxiety problems, and the relationship between anxiety and anger.

Chapter Five focuses on mood disorders, in particular, depression and bipolar disorder. This is an area in mental health where anger plays a central role. Using one's anger more effectively is almost always involved in reducing the level of pain as well as aiding in the recovery process.

Chapter Six examines addictions, a major way in which we misuse our anger. The relationship between this type of behavior and the original injury of deprivation of love is explored extensively. I hope that you will learn to look at deprivation versus empowerment, a central dynamic of addictions. In order to put out the fire of the dysfunctional anger of addiction, you have to be consciously aware of the decision to engage in addictive behavior.

Chapter Seven looks at relationships and emotional intimacy. In this chapter, you'll learn the definition of emotional intimacy and how to make your own relationship work. You'll learn how to build—or rebuild—trust as well as what poisons relationships. The same three steps to emotional success—the Stop, Drop, and Roll steps explained in Chapter Two—are used here to enable couples to learn effective conflict resolution and to improve their communication skills.

In Chapter Eight, I share my understanding of what is involved in fully healing the hole in your heart. This chapter describes in detail the process of healing in long-term therapy and clarifies what healing actually looks and feels like.

Chapter Nine is the conclusion, where the basics of the book are reviewed.

I hope you find this book to be helpful and I truly wish you all the love you could ever need to fill that dark and painful hole with soothing warmth and light.

# CHAPTER 1

# Why Is There a Hole in Your Heart?

## The Source of Anger

GEORGE THOUGHT HE WAS DYING. IN FACT, HE WISHED he would die, since it would be hard to imagine how he could be in more pain. He had already vomited several times and suffered from stomach cramps and severe nausea. He also had a migraine headache, complete with visual distortions and impaired vision. When he could see, he had vertigo; the room seemed like a ship at sea, swaying back and forth. He was hyperventilating and had severe chest pains, too. His wife, Melissa, called an ambulance.

George and Melissa were on their honeymoon in San Francisco. They had been married for all of forty-eight hours. He was twenty-seven.

When they arrived at the emergency room, the doctors couldn't identify anything wrong with George. He was extremely dehydrated, but he didn't respond to the intravenous fluids that they gave him. His symptoms were so severe, though, that they decided to admit him and run some tests.

After keeping George for a week, running extensive tests and spending almost $15,000, the doctors concluded that George was suffering from anxiety. He had experienced a severe panic attack.

The discovery of the hole in your heart and the beginning of your healing process don't have to begin with a panic attack. It might just be mild anxiety or nothing more than a dull ache, a feeling that you don't really belong. You may find yourself sinking down into the black hole of depression, where all light is absorbed by despair. Perhaps you find yourself unable to control your anger, exploding with people and feeling out of control. Maybe you find yourself unable to connect to your partner, or unable to even find a partner. Maybe you find yourself betraying your partner. You may notice that you're less able to keep from having another drink, no matter how you might try to deceive yourself. Or perhaps it was consuming that next line of cocaine, the extra box of cookies, or whatever form of pseudo-love you find yourself drawn to as part of your own personal nightmare.

What all of these difficulties have in common is that they are a result of anger being acted out in a dysfunctional way. Each represents the inability to use anger to fix what is really hurting you—your underlying emotional injury.

George, our honeymooner, learned this, too. Upon returning home, George began psychotherapy and found out that his panic attack was a way for his emotional being to get his attention about some serious concerns that he wasn't facing about his new marriage. He had been so out of touch with his own emotions that he had blocked out all of his misgivings about his wedding. So the only way his emotional being could get his attention was to make him utterly miserable. After all, beating yourself up with intense anxiety is an angry thing to do to yourself. However, George's emotional being seemed to have no other choice.

In therapy, George began to realize that he had gotten into a marriage that was, in many ways, a reenactment of some of the negative dynamics from his childhood. His new wife, Melissa, had a tendency to drink too much and had very loose boundaries. These behaviors were very similar to those of his mother. George had been oblivious to these problems until he finally got into treatment, thanks to his panic attack. His panic was an underlying angry reaction to emotional injuries that he had been ignoring. His panic attack forced him to deal with these problems.

This book was written to help you, like George, understand and deal with the emotional difficulties that are mostly a dysfunctional use of anger: depression, anxiety, relationship problems, explosive anger, passive-aggressive anger, and addictive behaviors. My hope is that by the time you have finished reading this book, you will understand why you are suffering—and also know that you can use the very same anger that has been fueling your dysfunction to begin to move toward healing.

## Injury and Healing

You might not expect a book about anger to talk about healing. But all problems, as well as all anger, begin with injury. Injuries need to be healed. Being injured causes pain, and pain is the original negative feeling.

There are three emotions that result from injury after the initial feeling of pain: sadness, fear, and anger. Sadness is a grieving of the injury. Just as we cry about the loss of a loved one, honoring our memory of them and their importance to us, we also mourn, in a smaller way, an injury to our self-esteem. For example, if we get a bad review at work, we may feel sad about it.

Fear, another response, is about not wanting to be hurt again. Just as we may become startled by a loud noise, our body generates energy in response to any injury to avoid being hurt again. Fear carries both energy and information that can be used to avoid further injury. Using the same example about a bad review at work, we may respond by becoming afraid that we may lose our job.

Anger, in contrast, is the natural healing energy that the body generates in order to attend to the injury. It would be reasonable to feel angry about receiving a bad review at work, whether it was justified or not. But how can you use that energy to fix the problem? If the anger is expressed directly—by blowing up at your boss, for example—you could lose your job. But that same anger may be used positively. For example, you could become more dedicated to working harder to get a better review in the next quarter.

While all of these responses to injury—sadness, fear, and anger—will be addressed in this book, the main focus will be on anger, the energy that is meant to heal.

## The Human Condition

Injury is part of the human condition. We are vulnerable. We all get injured. We all have holes in our hearts. It starts with being born and ends only, perhaps, in our passing. There is no escaping it.

So, you might ask, "If injury is inevitable, what's the point of trying to heal it?" The answer to that is what made you go into therapy or buy this book, and it's why we choose to have children. It's also why a tulip or daffodil bulb not only pushes up through compacted soil and reaches for the light, but goes beyond that to reveal itself in the glory of its flower.

We grow and move toward healing because of our pain and also because of our love of life. We grow and move toward healing because we know in our hearts that we deserve better than what we have received. Some people may even view this energy to heal, which I believe is generated by the unconscious, as a function of God. My personal belief is that God encompasses all that is, and therefore there is a part of God in all of us. Much of the work of psychotherapy may be seen as an attempt to contact and connect with that part of us.

For many years I resisted the idea that spirituality is important in psychotherapy. Having survived the experience of living in Boulder, Colorado, in the seventies and eighties, I saw many people use the concept of spirituality as a way to avoid dealing with the necessities of being moral human beings. They would use the idea of being on a spiritual path as an excuse to engage in all manner of destructive and angry behaviors. They would dismiss morality as "beneath" their high level of spirituality. In spite of having seen the term *spirituality* abused many times in my life, there clearly is an aspect of the spiritual in all healing. Again, I want to stress that my definition of spirituality includes a sense of morality. That means that what you do here, in your life, is important.

I want to clarify the term *unconscious* that I used above. So many words, like *spiritual* and *unconscious*, seem to be mystical and hard to pin down or understand. To make my meaning clear, when I use the word *unconscious* I mean that part of our selves that is present when we go to sleep. It is our body and that part of our minds that regulates our bodily functions that we do not consciously monitor. The unconscious heals our physical wounds, digests our food, and keeps us breathing while we are sleeping. Our *unconscious* keeps our hearts beating and cleans the poisons from our bodies. It nurtures our whole being, bringing nutrients to every cell in our bodies every day. It even speaks to us about the emotional dynamics of our lives by bringing dreams to our sleep.

But none of this really answers "Why do we have holes in our hearts?"

The obvious answer is that we all get injured in our childhoods. None of us has perfect parents who were able to anticipate our every need, set appropriate boundaries, and protect us from the plentiful injuries available out in the cold, cruel world. And, to add to what we are all up against, we have to realize that all of our parents come to us injured as well.

In fact, to really understand the impact of injury on our own personal human condition, we have to examine our place in the context the history of humanity. If you look at the maturation of humanity as a species, using the development of an individual as a metaphor, it's clear to me that humanity is in its adolescence, at best. As a species we continue to act in ways that compound the trauma that is a part of living.

If you have ever known anyone who has lost a parent at a young age, then you may understand the impact of that kind of trauma. Tremendous abandonment issues are likely to arise, even though it is obvious that parents usually don't die to get away from their children. Nonetheless, a parent's death is a serious emotional injury to any child.

Now, think about human history, where we have only just begun to scratch our way out of living in the mud. Diseases, which we have only begun to control in the last century, have taken many parents before their time. Currently, in America, the average life span is seventy to eighty years, but not very long ago those in their forties were considered to be ancient.

Think about the impact of famine, plague, and, especially, war on the emotional development of children. Those kinds of events bring the reality of life's difficulties into close focus very quickly. War creates an incredible amount of Post-Traumatic Stress Disorder, not only in the loss of parents, but in the rapes and torture that so frequently accompany the organized brutality of battle.

The tremendous impact of injuries like these on how we view other people and on our ability to trust and connect emotionally is simply overwhelming. But take it a step further: children who survive their various traumas usually become parents. These parents can be dysfunctional as a result of the impact of not just their own injuries, but also, in effect, the cumulative impact of all the centuries of wounding. Each injury leaves its emotional scars on the ongoing development of the collective human psyche.

Civilization represents humanity's attempt to make life fair. It is an extension of our feelings when we take seriously the responsibility of parenting. We want to provide comfort and protection to our children. We want them to have lives as good as or better than our own lives. We would like to prevent or heal their suffering. We would like to increase the joy in life for as many of us as possible. I've always seen Santa Claus, in a non-religious way, as the ultimate symbol of civilization. He—along with Mrs. Claus and the various and sundry elves—represents an adult's tremendous love and desire to make children happy.

In this light, it's clear to me that psychotherapy functions as the cutting edge of civilization. If civilization represents humanity's attempt to make life as fair as possible, given that it is not, then psychotherapy represents a person's attempt to heal from injuries which are, by definition, unfair. The more healed each person can become, the more likely he or she is able to function as a better parent. Thus, incrementally, one person at a time, mental health attempts to help civilization as a whole to mature and grow to a more effective and humane level.

Just like penicillin, the first true antibiotic, psychology is only about a hundred years old. Psychotherapy, which will always be more of a craft than a science, is the attempt to help people heal from their emotional injuries. It has been around for an even shorter period of time than antibiotics. In its current form, it has existed for, at most, fifty years. The art of psychotherapy continues to grow and progress as we learn new and different things from science about the brain, the body, and the functioning of the mind.

Years ago, in my first experience with orthopedic surgery, I saw a poster in the physician's office of a sapling tree with a broken branch that had been bent over. Its limb was wrapped, and a crutch had been put in place to support it in a more vertical position. The caption was something to the effect of "As the twig is bent, so grows the tree." Just as with any physical intervention or therapy, the central issue will continue to be how to heal the wounds of childhood. We also need to limit the ways that those injuries resonate and cause dysfunction into and through our adult lives.

There are various types of psychotherapy that can help an individual heal the hole in his heart. Long-term and short-term therapy can help address anger-related injuries. There is no clear boundary line between long-term and short-term psychotherapy. They are frequently interwoven. They both work on injury, though short-term therapy tends to work on more immediate problems and long-term therapy tends to focus more on healing childhood injuries. However, since current life struggles relate to the injuries of your childhood, you need to understand the connections between them, regardless of which type of therapy you are doing. This doesn't mean that everyone needs to do years and years of psychotherapy in order to have a good life. Some may need to, and others may want to, but it isn't mandatory.

Keep in mind that psychotherapy is costly, emotionally demanding, and time consuming. I always laugh when I hear managed care companies talking about how people who spend a long time in therapy are like Woody Allen, who they consider to be the poster child for what they call the "worried well." For most people, going to therapy is far more stressful than taking your car into the shop, and I don't know anyone who enjoys doing that every week. Just finding time in a busy and demanding life is a major hassle and the results of therapy are frequently a lot less concrete than having your fuel pump replaced.

But keep in mind that psychotherapy is a growth process, and the transition that takes place within an individual is one that takes time. This is part of what's problematic with much of today's managed care therapies that claim to be "solution-focused" therapy. Solution-oriented therapies in general can be valuable counseling techniques, very focused and helpful. However, they can be simplistic, frequently ignoring the impact of childhood injuries on the treatment process. When someone has issues with authority, as most of us do, there can be all kinds of resistance to the treatment process. If these dynamics are not addressed in the context of a safe and caring relationship, treatment will not succeed, no matter how focused it might be. Building a safe and caring relationship takes time, and that costs managed care companies money. Unfortunately, today, much of managed care is mostly focused on getting people out of therapy to save money for the administration and profits of insurance companies and/or their agents. True personal change, like developing relationships, takes time.

Short-term therapy, however, has its benefits. I think of short-term therapy as being focused more on solving problems in an immediate, day-to-day manner. If you want to quit smoking or if you're depressed, you usually don't want to sign up for years of therapy. You just want to get to a better place in your life as soon as possible.

The good news is that working on your problems in the here and now, while it usually requires an understanding of the connections to your past, doesn't require a full healing of your injuries. But doing short-term work in therapy does aid healing. As you work on the here-and-now aspects of your problems, you'll find out if you want or need to do that longer-term work and, if so, how much of it you want to do.

## Medication

Although I do not prescribe medications, I frequently refer clients to other doctors for medication as a part of their treatment. Medications can be very helpful in treatment, and at times are even necessary. This is true regardless of whether we're discussing mood disorders, anxiety problems, or explosive anger.

I have been amazed at how frequently clients resist recommendations to try medication. It has, on occasion, taken years for a client to accept my recommendation for a medication consultation. There are many reasons clients have for resisting medication. It makes them feel that they are "sick." Fears of side effects keep them from trying. Sometimes the client wants to avoid dependency.

All of the reasons and fears that clients can have about medication can be reasonable, yet the fact remains that many, many times the right medication can make a tremendous difference in speeding up the healing process and reducing the level of injury that clients experience in their lives. When an individual faces serious difficulties in his or her life, medication can be absolutely necessary. In these cases, clients need a psychiatrist, a medical doctor who specializes in mental health treatments.

If you have a treatment provider who is recommending that you consider medication, I would recommend that you take that advice seriously. It is quite reasonable to get a second opinion, but not reasonable to ignore the suggestion.

## What Is Anger?

While I have covered many topics we'll explore in this book, I have only written briefly about anger. Anger is the centerpiece of this book, and, as you may already realize, I like to be clear about the terms that I use. In this section, I will define anger in a way that is different from what most people understand that word to mean.

We all have trouble with anger. Anger, perhaps with the possible exception of sexual feelings, is probably the most troublesome emotion. It relates to the primitive aspects of our makeup. For most of us, anger is scary. Generally, people with anger hurt others, and none of us likes to be hurt.

However, we are all hurt by events in life. Did you ever notice that hurt and anger go together? The hurt comes first, followed by the anger. Men, in general, get in touch with their anger first, while women, in general, access their hurt feelings first. This is a result of both nature and nurture. The nature part relates to our genetic makeup. Some of us are more cognitively oriented, while others tend to be more emotionally oriented. In terms of the nurture issue, there is an androgyny split that takes place in us as we become socialized to one gender group when we grow up. Quite often, however, the standard sexual roles can be reversed, with men noticing their hurt feelings and women noticing their anger. With any particular injury, though, a single individual can respond with either anger or hurt. They may even show fear or sadness first.

My definition of anger is, as I said, significantly different than what most people think of when they hear the word. Most people associate anger with loud, scary, and bitter explosions. But I define anger as *the natural healing energy that the body generates in response to an injury*. This energy is meant to address or tend to the injury. For example, instead of blowing up at your boss after receiving a bad review, you can use the anger that surfaces to make your supervisor more aware of the good work you are doing. Or, you might want to dedicate some of that angry energy to doing a better job on your next project.

Actually, angry feelings and their expression occur along a spectrum. The stereotypical angry outburst falls on the red, hot end of the spectrum. In the middle, there is normal, assertive behavior, where people ask for what they want. There is also the blue, cold end of the spectrum, which is passive-aggressive anger.

Passive-aggressive anger is one of the most destructive interpersonal styles of behavior. The other, of course, is the aggressive behavior and violence, which are on the hot end of the spectrum. Both are very powerful interpersonal behaviors.

Passive-aggressive anger is based on the underlying premise of "You can't make me!" And that's true—we cannot make people *do* something. We can imprison them, and we can take their lives, but these actions do not necessarily elicit behaviors that we want from people.

In intimate relationships, passive-aggressive behavior can lead people to make agreements they won't keep. This then draws anger from their partner, based on the partner's injury of being disappointed. A classic example is when someone agrees to be somewhere at a certain time and then shows up late, making the other person wait. While passive-aggression often gets a bad rap, especially in relationships, you can see its power in that it is the basis of non-violent protest, such as that espoused by Gandhi and Martin Luther King Jr.

Anger, like fear, contains energy, which makes both emotions more action-oriented than sadness. Understanding that anger is an energy generated in response to an injury takes some of the negative feelings away from the experience of being angry. Realizing that it isn't bad or destructive to have these kinds of emotions provides the opportunity to be thoughtful and proactive about how to use this energy to fix what is hurting you. The energy of anger is meant to *empower* you to solve the problems and heal the injuries in your life.

## What Is Power?

Power is the use of energy to act on the world so that it meets your needs. This energy frequently comes from anger when we are responding to an injury. This is a simple concept, but one that is frequently lost on many of us in our attempts to cope with the world.

Most of us don't have to think about responding to a mosquito. The natural response is to swat it and flick the squashed creature off of your body. Most people wouldn't think that swatting the mosquito is a use of power. This simple example, of experiencing an injury and using the resulting anger in an appropriate use of power, demonstrates the way that we deserve to function when we experience emotional or physical injury.

When something is hurting us we have a natural tendency to respond in a manner that takes care of and protects us. This same, simple process is distorted in most problems involving mental health. Instead of simply using anger to fix what is hurting us, we end up behaving in ways that cause us further harm. To think of it in terms of the mosquito example, it would be like slapping yourself—not the mosquito. It's amazing how often we do just that. In my experience, people seeking help in psychotherapy have problems that are related to this central concept. By this I mean to include problems with depression, anxiety, addiction, and emotional intimacy.

This distorted response to injury begins with faulty learning in childhood. We learn ways of responding and coping for our very survival. We begin life as completely dependent beings and we learn our lessons about emotions, intimacy, and power from our parents: adults who typically are injured and have created a dysfunctional family environment. Many of us don't begin to realize our own, internalized dysfunction until we leave home. I call this learning process the *loss of innocence*. We may lose our innocence when we run into some major difficulty, such as depression, anxiety, divorce, addiction, or problems with the law.

Leaving home and the protection of our family of origin is a major developmental step, one that can be quite intimidating. Even if it is dysfunctional, the family is known, and, therefore, is safer than the unknown. To prepare for this transition, I believe we put on our emotional and body armor and assume the *mantle of innocence*, which I view as the basic assumption we make about our intrinsic "OK-ness," or acceptability to others. When we're wearing our mantle of innocence, we assume that all will be "fine" and that we are "fine" as we take that leap of faith and enter the cold, cruel world outside the family of origin.

Losing our innocence, while quite painful emotionally, is the beginning of the movement to maturity. We reach a level of maturity when we can deal with the injuries in our childhood in a way that keeps them from continuing to interfere with our current lives. In order to reach such a place of healing, however, we have to learn to deal effectively with our anger. This can be challenging because of the misunderstandings and negative lessons we learn about angry emotions from both dysfunctional family environments and society in general.

## What Is Intimacy?

Emotional intimacy is one of the most difficult things to accomplish because it requires being able to accept all of the feelings of another person, even if you don't like those feelings. It requires us to accept our partner's feelings even when they don't make sense to us. It also requires that our partners accept our feelings unconditionally, too. But when we have learned inappropriate ways of dealing with our feelings, as almost all of us have, it can lead to a lot of conflict and lack of intimacy.

Oftentimes we struggle with intimacy because we've learned dysfunctional things about anger. We often experience a double bind in dealing with our angry feelings. This explains, metaphorically, why we end up slapping ourselves in the face instead of swatting the mosquito. The double bind of interpersonal anger starts when you're angry about something. You see your choices as either expressing that anger and being rejected for doing so, or not expressing it, and therefore not getting your needs met. Part of the difficulty involved with this process is the way in which people express—or don't express—their angry feelings.

Anger has a spectrum to it. Most people are used to defining anger as only the hot or violent end of the spectrum. The other extreme is the cold and distant or withdrawn response. Most people don't see or consider the rainbow of gradations in the center of the spectrum, which includes lots of normal, assertive behaviors.

The interpersonal challenge, especially in our most intimate relationships, is to realize that your anger, and that of those around you, can be a gift. It is a gift because you could choose to leave or not share your pain and anger, which eventually causes more emotional distance. It's not a gift if you're stuck with depression, or overreacting with explosive anger, or withdrawing from those around you. However, if you can accept your own anger and learn how to express it effectively while accepting the difficult feelings of those around you, you're making the power of those intense feelings start to work for you.

Gradually, with conscious attention, work, and courage, these new emotional behaviors will begin to dispel the feelings of helplessness generated by that double bind. To break the double bind of anger means learning that your choices of angry behaviors are not limited to either stuffing your anger or exploding. You will find that the difficult feelings can be expressed outward, to others, with the results that you desire. As your skill increases, you will find more success with those you love, and find others who are interested in and capable of accepting your emotions.

# CHAPTER 2

# How to Unbend Your Anger

## *Stop, Drop, and Roll*

GEORGE'S STORY DIDN'T END IN AN EMERGENCY ROOM during his honeymoon. When George and his new wife, Melissa, returned home to Chicago from San Francisco, he went about making changes in his life. George began taking an antidepressant medication prescribed by his psychiatrist to address his anxiety long term and he also took tranquilizers to address any panic attacks. He also began seeing a psychotherapist, Alan Hastings, a licensed marriage and family counselor, to address the psychological aspects of his panic attack.

Alan quickly realized that George was out of touch with his own feelings. George, an only child, was raised by his mother, Marilyn, an alcoholic who was depressed. Marilyn demanded a lot from William, her husband. Marilyn was depressed after George was born and continued to struggle with alcohol. She was functional, however, and worked after she and William divorced when George was less than two years old. At first, William was involved with George, but less so when, a year later, he remarried and started a new family. This left George to take care of Marilyn's sloppy, drunken behavior and her sour, bitter, and demanding demeanor. George could never be good enough for her.

After a few meetings, his therapist, Alan, explained to George how the panic attack on his honeymoon related to the injury of Melissa's heavy drinking during their first night in San Francisco. When Melissa had gotten pretty inebriated, she slurred her words and was loud. This embarrassed George, who nonetheless took very good care of her. He had gotten her back to the hotel and into bed, where she promptly fell asleep. The next morning, at breakfast, she had a Bloody Mary, and shortly afterwards George experienced his panic attack and went to the hospital.

Alan clarified George's injuries on his honeymoon. Here they were, married and celebrating in San Francisco, and Melissa became unavailable and needy on their second night of marriage. Then, the very next morning, she began to drink again.

Alan talked about how George might feel about these injuries. They explored normal feelings of sadness, fear, and anger that follow an injury. Alan discussed how George's fear of having to take care of Melissa—just as he had taken care of his mother—might have made him sad and afraid that he was returning to an endless caretaking role. Alan talked about how George was probably angry about Melissa's behavior, and the way in which that anger, along with his old anger about his father's and mother's abandonment, combined to exaggerate his fears, causing his panic attack. Alan talked about how George's emotional being finally got his attention through this process.

Alan and George began to focus on ways to help George get in touch with himself emotionally and to work toward preventing any further panic attacks. Alan said that he wanted George to avoid any further panic by using tranquilizers at the first sign of anxiety, until he started to get the benefit of the longer-acting antidepressant medication. Though they frequently referenced the way in which George's current life was reenacting injuries from his childhood, their focus was mostly on what was happening in the present and recent past for George. They worked to take back George's anger, use it for empowerment, and keep it from exaggerating his fears.

## Stop, Drop, and Roll

As George discovered, understanding your anger can help you get to the root of your injury. One technique I've developed for clients to do just this is "Stop, Drop, and Roll." It is a system, a process to help you to identify your anger and "unbend" it.

The idea of *bent anger* may seem kind of strange. Consider, however, my definition of anger: the natural healing energy that the body produces in response to an injury. If anger isn't used to fix what is hurting you, it will be "bent" into some dysfunctional use of your anger. Bent anger, then, means anger which is dysfunctional. The Stop, Drop, and Roll technique will help you redirect your anger.

Stop, Drop, and Roll will help you to unbend your anger so that you can use it to empower or nurture you. Learning this system will help you to take major, as well as minor, problems and reduce their impact on your life. Unbending your anger using this technique will change the direction that your anger flows, so that it moves away from neurotic, self- (and other-) abusive behaviors. If you think back to the metaphor of the mosquito, you'll learn how to stop slapping yourself in the face and get that bloodsucking insect instead.

I call my system Stop, Drop, and Roll because it's easy to remember, and it's what you're supposed to do when you are on fire. Before you can Stop, Drop, and Roll, however, you first have to notice that you are on fire. This means identifying the dysfunctional way your anger is being expressed. It may be expressed in exaggerating your fears into anxiety or panic. It may be expressed, on the cold end of the anger spectrum, by distancing yourself from people you care about who injure you emotionally. Perhaps you express it by overeating or drinking too much. You might pretend that nothing bothers you at all. You might find yourself flirting with someone else while you're married, or even considering having an affair. There are an infinite number of ways to strike yourself, and those you care about, without even realizing you're doing it.

After you begin to notice that you are on fire, you can *Stop*, which means taking time out and stepping back from the immediacy of the fire; *Drop* to the ground, or get grounded, which is the task of understanding your injuries and emotions; and *Roll*, which is the action step in which you will begin to use the energy of your anger functionally.

Not only does the Stop, Drop, and Roll system help you unbend your anger, but it also gets you in touch with an aspect of what psychologists call an *ego state*. An ego state refers to the psychological fact that, depending on how you're functioning at any point in time, you may be acting as either a child, adult, or parent might behave. For example, anytime we're being playful we are in a Child ego state. That might be making jokes, singing, or dancing. In addition, if you are experiencing any strong negative emotion, you are likely functioning in your "Hurt" Child ego state. If you are planning where to go on vacation this summer or how to pay your bills, you are likely in an Adult ego state. If you are listening to your partner explain his or her upset emotional state or discussing how much allowance to give your child, you are likely functioning in a "Good" Parent ego state.

Each step also corresponds to an aspect of Body, Mind, and Spirit. I think of the Body aspect as resonating with the more primitive, Child ego state. In this state we are more emotional, which is a more physical experience than thinking. The Mind aspect corresponds to the Adult ego state, where we are thinking about what is going on for us, both in the here and now as well as in the past. The Spirit aspect is similar to the "Good" Parent ego state in that it represents taking the energy of anger and using it to connect with love and caring, expressing those positive aspects in healing and caretaking actions.

While the Stop, Drop, and Roll system is easy to understand, accomplishing each step requires a great deal of effort, and each step can be difficult for different reasons and for different people.

The first step—Stop—requires that you identify and recognize that you're on fire, meaning that you can spot problematic thoughts, feelings, or behaviors before they become overwhelming. Once you recognize that you're on fire you need to Stop or take a "time out." Both of these pieces of the Stop step are not easy to do for a variety of reasons.

You'd think that it would be easy to notice if you were on fire, but we're talking about habitual and frequently unconscious behaviors. It can take a while to train yourself to notice these behaviors once you've identified them.

Stopping, or taking time out, can be difficult because

whether you know it or not, whenever you are experiencing self-abusive thoughts or dysfunctional emotions (i.e., anxiety or depression), you are in a Hurt Child ego state. When you are in this ego state, it feels painful to be abandoned, to take a time out instead of receiving the nurturing you need. The pain causes people to resist changing to another ego state, either Adult or Parent. But, over time, completing the steps and changing ego states will bring nurturing to the Hurt Child in the Roll step.

With practice, being able to notice that you're on fire will become easier. The completion of the entire process will help the Hurt Child to trust being left temporarily. But trust usually takes time to establish. It has to be earned by going through the full cycle.

Another reason that the first step can be hard is that emotions are both chemical (biological) and psychological. In fact, most neuropsychologists believe that this last statement is similar to the famous chicken-and-egg debate. They just don't see a distinction between the biological and the psychological. Just as various chemical compounds—medications, drugs, etc.—can impact our emotional state, so can therapeutic interventions. Psychotherapy (as well as the rest of our experience) changes brain chemistry. Memories are stored electrobiochemically.

Once you are feeling overwhelmed by a negative emotion (such as anxiety, which is fueled by adrenaline, also known as epinephrine), a certain amount of time will be needed for the body to process the higher levels of the chemical out of your system. In order to prevent the production of these stimulating chemicals, it is necessary to identify the problematic thought, feeling, or behavior very early in the process, before uncomfortable amounts of the chemicals are produced in your body. To accomplish this, you need to be in touch with yourself physically and emotionally, and to train yourself to be on the lookout for problematic thoughts, feelings, or behaviors. You must develop your own early warning system, which is basically the first part of the first step, so that you notice when you are on fire.

Not everyone has equal difficulty with all of the steps. Some people who are already quite in touch with their feelings may find it easy to get to the second step. On the other hand, people who are already highly cognitive and out of touch emotionally may have difficulty with the first step and find the second step easier.

It's important to appreciate all of the effort you make in putting this easy-to-learn but difficult-to-do process to work for you. Each time you make an attempt to do things differently, it is a success. Keep in mind that a therapist can be either helpful or indispensable in helping you to keep the overall perspective and continuity in your growth process. Frequently the need to have a therapist involved depends on the level of injury you carry with you from your childhood. However you proceed, you're making progress if you're making an effort.

## My Own Story

Here's an example of how the Stop, Drop, and Roll process worked for me. When I was in my twenties, I was struggling with depression and anxiety. I was also a pretty good handball player. I signed up to play in a tournament although I struggled somewhat with anxiety about performing well in it. Unfortunately, I lost a match to another pretty good player, even though I'd felt that I should have been able to beat him.

Afterwards, as I left the gymnasium, I noticed that I was starting to get depressed. I felt that black, sinking feeling in my chest and I was thinking negative thoughts. When I noticed this, I was able to sort of emotionally back up. I took a time out and looked at what had happened. My usual response would have been to spend several hours—or even a couple of days—in a sour, depressed state. Since it was a Friday, it could have ruined my whole weekend. Instead, I was able to realize that losing the match was not the end of the world and wouldn't destroy my weekend. Later, I called my opponent and arranged for a non-tournament rematch and won.

Here's how I used the Stop, Drop, and Roll system:

• Stop: I noticed my early signs of depression—my black thoughts and that horrible sinking feeling in my chest. I was in the Hurt Child ego state and was consumed by the pain of losing the match. My depression represented my anger about losing. I was turning it against myself, telling myself that I wasn't OK.

• Drop: After noticing my body's signals, I grounded myself by getting into the Adult ego state. I distanced myself from the event and investigated what happened. I became cognitve and thoughtful, and reviewed my response to losing the match. I realized that my response was depressive, and, therefore, angry. I thought about other times I had felt like this.

• Roll: After I got over my immediate reactions, I began to think about what I could do differently with my anger. I decided not to give in to that depressive mood. I told myself it wasn't the end of the world. Finally, I called my opponent for a rematch and to get closure on the situation.

Going through the entire process—Stop, Drop, and Roll—helped me act as a Good Parent to nurture my Hurt Child. I used the energy of anger effectively, transforming the anger from anxiety and depression into power or self-nurturance. I unbent and redirected the energy of anger into attending to the injury.

To act as a Good Parent means that you nurture the Hurt Child within you by exercising power, by acting and using the angry energy functionally. It may be that you confront what is causing the pain or that you engage in some self-nurturing activity. The challenge is to discover the action that will best take care of your injured Child at that point in time, and then put it into practice.

Playing the role of Good Parent to your Hurt Child is the completion of the Body, Mind, and Spirit triangle. The Spirit is represented in the caretaking that the Good Parent delivers to the injured Body—the Hurt Child—after having been thoughtful about the injury in the Mind or Adult state. The Good Parent is the essence of being spiritual in terms of delivering your love, either to yourself or to others.

When you have completed these steps successfully, you will, in effect, have "unbent" the healing energy of anger. It will no longer be used to hurt your self or someone else in some neurotic manner. It will be directed into either empowering you by acting on the world in some way that insures that the world nurtures you, or by directly nurturing your self.

The sections below explain and demonstrate each step in greater detail to help you develop a better understanding of them.

### Step One: Notice You're On Fire and Stop!
### "I feel, therefore I am!"

The great philosopher Rene Descartes wrote about how to begin to understand and cope with life. The first step he could think of was to validate his own existence by validating his own awareness. His most famous quote is *"Cogito, ergo sum,"* or, "I think, therefore I am."

However, many of us have more trouble dealing with our feelings than dealing with our thoughts. I chose to subtitle this section "I feel, therefore I am" to draw attention to how we undervalue our emotions. Many of us have been so conditioned to disregard our emotions that the idea of validating our existence by validating our feelings seems totally foreign.

Although we tend to undervalue our feelings, being aware of them before they become overwhelming is critical to taking control of the problems in our lives. This means identifying the problematic thoughts, feelings, or behaviors when they are *not* happening.

Many people struggle with anger without realizing they are doing so. It's obvious that people are struggling with anger when it looks like the conventional definition of anger. When someone is experiencing explosive anger, it's not hard to identify. But losing one's temper isn't the only type of angry behavior.

Passive-aggressive anger, on the cold end of the spectrum, is just the opposite of what we typically think of as anger. People who are passive-aggressive express their anger by *not* doing things they agree to do and drawing the anger of others toward themselves. They can even get indignant at the anger of others that they have caused: "Why are you so *angry* all the time?"

Another angry behavior that doesn't look angry is addiction. Addictive behaviors don't look angry except in the way the person is injuring themselves. Depression doesn't always look angry either, since it is self-directed.

What is the problematic anger-based thought, feeling, or behavior that troubles you?

Identifying these feelings can help you to develop your own early-warning system, which is vitally important because of the chemical nature of emotions. Since emotions are communicated in the body chemically, we want to stop the production of these chemicals as soon as possible. The early warning system can help you to stop the body from manufacturing and pumping the chemicals that produce higher levels of distress.

The following exercise can be quite helpful in training yourself to be able to notice that you are on fire.

---

### Exercise to Develop Your Early Warning System

Try this exercise to develop your early warning system so that you can begin to learn to unbend your anger and start healing yourself.

•Identify your problematic thoughts, feelings, or behaviors. Make a list, and eventually prioritize the items, starting with the ones that you want to deal with first. Your list could include explosive anger, depressive thoughts or feelings, anxiety, avoidant behaviors, unspoken resentments in your relationship, or cravings for some addictive substance or behavior.

•Once you have focused on your most pressing problem (you can come back to the others), try to remember the last time it occurred. If you have difficulty, choose the time that comes most easily to your memory. It could be the last time you erupted in anger and had a fight with your partner. Perhaps it was the last time you felt anxious in a social setting. Or it could be the last time you noticed thinking that you were worthless.

•Now, concentrate on the beginning of that experience. Did you notice it first in your body as a physical or emotional sensation, or as a problematic or negative thought? Do you remember the beginning of a problematic behavior? Whatever you have identified, you can now develop your focus and make a target to concentrate on. It may be a visualization of the behavior. If it is a feeling, imagine that feeling as a physical manifestation. Give it a color, a shape, and/or an identity. If it's a thought, visualize it written or typed on a piece of paper.

•Now that you have this image in your mind's eye, practice zooming in and out on it. Imagine that you're so close to it that you would experience it as if you were a fly on a photograph. Walk all around it and get familiar with it. Then pull way back and see the photograph diminish to a dot. Imagine that it's like a slide, and you can go around the back of it and see it in reverse. If your focus is a thought, hear it in your own voice. Now speed it up so that it seems very high pitched and squeaky. Slow it down so that the pitch is low. Then imagine hearing someone you like saying it. Then hear someone you don't like saying that thought. The idea is to become so sensitized to the targeted problem that the next time it occurs, you won't miss it.

•Now that you have the problem clearly in focus, hold onto the original image and think the words, "WARNING! WARNING! PROBLEM APPROACHING!" Hear these words at high volume. You may remember the *Star Trek* episodes with the sirens and the red lights flashing an alert and conjure up that image. Perhaps you will associate it with police or ambulance sirens. It can be any alarm that fits for you as long as it's an annoying and continuing sound. Then turn it off by thinking "TIME OUT!"

•Practice this step on your own, at least once per day, for two weeks, or until you feel that your early-warning system is in place.

•Feel free at any time to put the Stop step into practice by taking a time out when your early-warning system works.

---

This exercise helps you pay attention to your physical and emotional body. Whether the problem is focused on difficult thoughts, feelings, or behaviors, the underlying problem is emotional in nature. The fact that you may not experience the problem as a difficult emotion doesn't mean that the source of the problem isn't emotional. It is! Being in touch with your feelings is of primary importance in this first step. Your early-warning system is based on noticing that you are on fire, which you can't do if you're out of touch emotionally.

Life problems are almost always a function of emotions, even when the problems are not as obvious as when they relate directly to anxiety, depression, or explosive expressions of anger. Here are three situations that don't necessarily look like emotional problems until you look beneath the surface.

If we look at someone suffering with an addiction, it may not be obvious that this relates to emotional problems. Although I'll discuss this in more detail in Chapter Six, let's take a brief look at what addictions are about. Addictions are when someone engages in a repeated self-destructive behavior, and *feels* that they lack the ability to change that behavior. Whether we are talking about drug or alcohol addiction, sex addiction, food addiction, cigarette smoking, or something else, the reality is that the person addicted doesn't have to continue to engage in the problematic behavior. However, they *feel* compelled to continue the behavior, even when they agree and understand that the behavior is self-destructive. Self-destructive behavior is a way to be very angry with yourself. You can see that we have already addressed the word *feel* two times in describing addictions, as well as the word *anger*, an emotion.

What about when someone who is married and having an affair? This may not seem to be an emotional decision. Perhaps it appears that the person having the affair is just being selfish or self-indulgent. Perhaps they can justify it based on extenuating circumstances, like "My wife doesn't love me." It may seem to be a rational decision, based on the logic that if my wife doesn't love me I have the right to seek affection elsewhere. However, when we look at the words *selfish* or *self-indulgent*, we see, again, words that carry a negative emotional judgment. There is also the fact that when someone has an affair, they are betraying their wedding vows. Breaking the marital contract is an angry behavior.

Another example would be someone who can't stop thinking negative thoughts about himself. This kind of behavior would mean that he was probably suffering from low self-esteem. This type of thinking may not seem to be involved with any particular emotion when you look at it superficially. Thinking something like "I'll never amount to anything" may appear to be simply a thought. But added up over time, those thoughts may lead to serious depression and/or anxiety.

When we look a bit more closely at this type of negative thinking, however, it becomes obvious that it is an angry behavior. If you told a friend "You'll never amount to anything," it would hurt their feelings and might even draw anger back at you. It's amazing how often we say these mean and abusive kinds of thoughts to ourselves and never realize how angry they are. This anger is almost always tied to early childhood injuries as well as current injuries and isn't meant to be directed against ourselves. It is meant to be used to heal those injuries whether they are in the present or from childhood.

There is anger involved in all of these examples. Problems with anger underlie the vast majority of emotional difficulties. By thinking about the examples above, you can begin to see how emotions are entangled in every problematic thought, feeling, or behavior that we might like to address.

## Getting in Touch with Your Emotions

I find that most people who have emotional problems are not in touch with their own feelings. That isn't surprising, since men dominate our culture, and men have been conditioned to avoid their feelings. But whatever your gender, if you are out of touch with your feelings it has probably resulted from a combination of both nature and nurture. By this I mean that people are likely to feel their emotions more or less strongly based to some extent on genetic factors. People who feel them more strongly tend to value emotions. People who feel them less strongly tend to value thinking. That's the nature part. The nurture part comes from the way in which parents and society raise us. This also has a major impact on how we develop the skill of being in touch emotionally.

When we are infants, and even as we begin to grow, our parents are giants who hold the power of life and death in their hands. Initially, at least, we depend on them for everything. This position makes what they say and feel tremendously important to our survival. Regardless of how our genetics may influence us, we need their love, approval, and protection to survive. If they let us know (either verbally or non-verbally) that emotion is not acceptable, then we will have two options. One option is that we accept that direction and become distant from what we feel. We become "Good" Kids. We are likely to become more focused on thoughts than feelings. However, there is another option. If we reject the parental demand to ignore emotion, we are likely to become "Bad"

Kids. "Bad" Kids are more rebellious as children, more emotionally expressive and less reserved. Whatever way you developed, one challenge of the first step is to know what you are feeling. If you are more emotionally expressive, you will probably have an easier time doing that.

Emotions are not something to be judged. When we see something, we may not like what we are looking at, but we don't tell ourselves that we shouldn't see what we see. That is the metaphor I like for feelings. Emotions contain information about how we need to take care of ourselves in the world, especially interpersonally. They also bring us energy. Our feelings demand understanding.

Most people think that emotions are irrational. I like to tell people that emotions are not irrational. They are non-rational. Emotions always make sense. They are logical once you accept them. If you accept your emotions you can always learn to understand and make sense out of them. You will find them quite helpful in guiding your decisions about the emotional side of your life. For most of us, that means your entire interpersonal life.

So, how does someone develop the skill of being in touch with what they are feeling, especially when they have been trained to not know what they are feeling? Developing the skill of getting in touch emotionally is just like developing any other skill you might want to acquire. You must learn the basics and practice over and over again. However, the skill of getting in touch emotionally is much less concrete than other skills. When you learn to swing a tennis racket a certain way or to use a new computer program, you can get concrete external feedback very quickly. Emotions take place within a person and are less easily observed, and therefore less concrete. This does not make them any less real, however.

You can do various activities to develop this important skill. The first thing that I recommend to clients is that they begin by asking themselves the question "What am I feeling right now?" over and over again on a daily basis. I recommend that each individual who is trying to develop this skill plan out how many times per day to ask themselves that question. It can be three or six or twenty. It can be every time you eat or every time you go to the bathroom. There is a right approach for each individual, and you need to find the one that is right for you.

The key is to try to avoid *figuring out* what you're feeling—just listen for an answer. People who are very out of touch emotionally frequently lack an immediate answer to the question of what they're feeling. Keep asking it anyway.

The second thing I recommend is to write in a journal about the experiences you have during this process. This helps to stay in touch with your subjective experiences and gives an extra focus to tracking your emotions. It also will help you to observe yourself as your skills develop.

If you have trouble accessing any emotion at all after a couple of weeks of asking the question "What am I feeling right now?" try scanning your body for any areas of muscle tension or discomfort. If you find a tense area, close your eyes and try to send your consciousness into that part of your body. Then, speak as that part of your body about what is going on. Tell yourself, from that place, what you are feeling. If this still doesn't bring anything to the surface, then, and only then, you can try to figure out what you are feeling. Recording this process in your journal can be helpful.

What you should experience over the first few months of getting in touch with your emotions is that you begin to recognize what you are feeling on a more regular basis. This will be helpful in all of the three steps—Stop, Drop, and Roll—but especially in the first step.

## James' Story

The experience of James can help to make it clear how to use the Stop, Drop, and Roll system on a problem relating to anger. James is a twenty-six-year-old carpenter who does production framing for one of the three largest builders in Denver. His father, Earl, had a small business in the building trades. Earl liked to drink beer, but kept his habit in check. James' mother, Myra, was a full-time housewife who raised four children.

James was youngest of the boys. His oldest brother, Junior, was seven years older than Steve, who was only fourteen months older than James. James, in turn, was two years older than Rebecca, the youngest. Myra was pregnant with Junior when she and Earl were married two years out of high school. They had had some difficult times early in their marriage and they weren't sure that it would last. However, they got through those times because they loved each other, even though they weren't especially affectionate. They also loved their kids.

Myra was occasionally mildly depressed during the early years with the kids. Junior was kind of independent, like his father, but Steve and James were both very close and very competitive. They got into lots of physical fights as boys and as teens. Steve was a lot bigger than James and an angry young man. Steve felt as if he couldn't compete with Junior for his father's attention and took out his anger by dominating James in as many ways as he could.

James was at the bottom of the parental attention list. Myra was worn out from keeping up with the kids and trying to keep Steve from teasing and abusing James.

James had developed problems with explosive anger in high school. He was generally quieter than Steve, but he would lose it when he was really frustrated, turning red in the face and becoming belligerent and threatening whoever was around him. Afterwards, when he had settled down, he always had mixed feelings about the explosion. On the one hand, he felt better for having released the pent-up tension. He also enjoyed the fact that it made others back away and leave him alone. On the other hand, he was embarrassed by his outbursts.

After high school, both Junior and Steve worked at their father's business, but James was desperate to get away from his family. He moved out immediately after graduation and married his high school sweetheart, Alice, a year later. James worked as a carpenter, while Alice worked in a real estate office doing clerical work and supporting the brokers and agents. Alice wasn't too concerned about James' angry outbursts, since they were never directed at her, and she figured that the problem would just go away as soon as James got away from his family, especially Steve.

Of course, James' problem with anger didn't just go away, though it did recede into the background for awhile. The first few years that James and Alice were married and building their life together, James' anger was less of a problem. It would show up at work at times, when another construction worker would tease him, but it was pretty infrequent. Also, James had as little to do with his family as possible and avoided them whenever he could.

After James and Alice had been married for a couple of years, and Alice had become assistant office manager in the real estate office, they decided to have kids. James wanted Alice to stay at home like his mother had, but they just couldn't swing it financially. They had used Alice's position and income to find a good deal on a starter home and get a loan. They couldn't make their house payments on just James' income.

The stress started to mount in their lives with the birth of their son, Tim, and increased two years later with the addition of their daughter, Theresa. As the stress of having children increased, the frequency of James' angry outbursts did too. Eventually, after an incident at work caused James to lose his job, Alice convinced him to seek counseling.

James would learn to use the Stop, Drop, and Roll system in his psychotherapy, but you could say, in an overall way, that he had completed the Stop step when he entered therapy. He—or Alice—noticed that he was on fire, that he had a problem with explosive anger. He had agreed to go to treatment, which would give him a chance to take a time out from the day-to-day cycle of injury followed by explosions followed by guilt and withdrawal. Soon, he would begin the second step in his process.

## Step Two: Drop! Getting Grounded
### "I think, therefore I can!"

Getting lost is an upsetting and difficult experience. If you don't have directions, you need to stop and get your bearings. That is what the second step—Drop—is all about. The first step allowed you to recognize that you were on fire. You were able to take a time out before you got overwhelmed so that you wouldn't get completely lost. Now that you have the time to reflect on your situation, you're ready for the second step.

The Drop step is based on understanding what is going on. You know that you are experiencing a problematic thought, feeling, or behavior that's linked to your emotions. But to achieve a full understanding of the problem, there are a number of questions that you need to ask yourself to help clarify your situation.

The first question is "What is going on right now that has caused this to happen?" This connects your most recent experience to your current round of emotional difficulty. It could be something someone said or how they treated you. This could remind you of a previous difficult experience.

You can get more specific about understanding the feelings involved in this current problem, as well as any old injuries, by asking yourself these additional questions:

- "What is hurting me right now and how does this relate to the past?"

- "What am I angry about right now and how does this relate to the past?"

- "What am I afraid of right now and how does this relate to the past?"

- "What am I sad about right now and how does this relate to the past?"

Don't be concerned if you don't have answers to these questions. Keep asking them and thinking about them. In time, you will receive answers.

The concept of *transference* can help us sort out the role of the past in our current emotional difficulties. That is why the questions relate to the present and the past. Transference is frequently called "old business," or the way in which the emotional injuries of our childhood may resonate and contribute emotional charge or power to our current emotional injuries.

An example of how transference can begin to be recognized is included in George's story. If you think back to George's panic attack, his pain, fear, and anger about his wife's drinking and dependency was compounded by his old unresolved feelings about his mother's drinking and dependency. Those angry feelings combined to pile ontop of his fears and produce a major panic experience.

Transference happens all the time for everyone in every relationship to varying degrees. When these feelings become strong enough, they can interfere in our relationships in major and minor ways.

Untangling transference dynamics in our relationships is challenging. It takes a great deal of self-awareness to be able to notice the impact of those old feelings on our current relationships. Working at that is part of the experience of working on Stop, Drop, and Roll.

## James' Story Continues

James' anger problem had reached a critical point when he was fired from his job and Alice persuaded him to go to counseling. James wasn't very happy about going; he didn't believe in it, nor did he think that it would help. He said that he went to make Alice happy, but secretly he hoped for some relief.

He was pleasantly surprised to find that he liked his counselor, Sam. He had some anxiety about it, but after the first session he settled down. Sam helped James to begin to understand why he suffered from his angry outbursts.

While James was in the counseling sessions, he wasn't actively upset. He had identified his emotional problem as explosive anger. With Sam's help, he was beginning to do the Drop step, the second step to achieving emotional success: he was thinking about his problems. Sam and James developed an understanding of James' difficulties related to his childhood injuries. They decided that James' lack of attention from his father, his brother Steve's abuse, and his mother's lack of protection all were part of the old injuries. These old emotional injuries were supplying the extra anger that was fueling his outbursts.

They also looked at the things that set James off in the here and now. The provocation was almost always a conflict at work— for example, when someone was teasing him or questioning his judgment. James experienced these things as injuries in the here and now, and he responded to them with defensiveness and anger.

Sam and James then explored the way in which those present injuries related to his old injuries. James could see that when he felt abused by a male coworker, all of his old experiences with Steve were brought to the surface. All of those feelings of being put down and abused in the past would mix in with the feelings he was having in his present conflict.

They also explored the way in which the current stress in James' life added to his sense of injury. Any injury can move someone into the Hurt Child ego state. The sleep deprivation that goes along with having children, as well as the lack of attention from Alice, were other here-and-now injuries that caused James to live with a higher level of frustration. Alice's increased distance also resonated with his feelings of abandonment by his mother during childhood. James was uncomfortable to realize that he was jealous of the attention his kids got from Alice, which reminded him of how he wasn't attended to as well as he needed to be by his own mother.

James was both amazed and relieved by figuring out these

things. It helped to have his counselor, Sam, put things in perspective. He was amazed to realize how much was going on emotionally, inside of himself. He had been completely unaware of all of these emotions and old injuries, and was relieved to realize that all of these emotions were normal feelings that anyone would have in his situation. He no longer felt like some crazy, out-of-control person.

James also learned that it was OK to have the feelings that he was having, even if some of them were "ugly." Ugly feelings are those that are not socially acceptable, and include anger, fear, jealousy, envy, and even sadness. On some level, no negative feelings are socially acceptable. However, they are just feelings, and, in reality, they are acceptable by definition. That means simply that you are allowed to feel what you feel, regardless of what anyone else might tell you.

Having Sam there as his counselor to validate that his feelings were just feelings, and OK to have, helped James to become more accepting of his own emotions. The relationship James was developing with Sam also benefited from a positive transference. James was finally getting attention from a caring male authority figure, which added a soothing and healing impact to their counseling sessions.

The contrast between James' relationship with Sam and James' relationship with his father was both helpful and painful at times. It helped that the caring attention James received was like a soothing balm on a raw wound. The problem was that it reminded him of the pain of abandonment he had experienced with his father, Earl. At times, early on in treatment, James would get angry with Sam for no apparent reason. When James felt comfortable enough to bring this up with Sam, they quickly figured out the transference involved. Doing so reassured James that his emotions really did make sense.

This example shows what the second step, the Drop step, is all about. James was able to work on the first step both inside and outside of therapy. He was able to also address the cognitive, Adult task in the second step in therapy, where he was able to be thoughtful and reflective. In his sessions, he had the chance to ask and answer the four questions of the Drop step with the help of his therapist, Sam.

You may wonder how you can accomplish this without the help of a therapist. The answer is to work with the questions on your own, using this example, as well as the others in this book, as a guide. There is no doubt that having a good, supportive counselor or therapist makes the process easier. However, in many situations, you can do these steps on your own.

A journal also is a tremendously helpful tool in tracking your process. Keep in mind the questions themselves and give yourself permission to have the feelings that you have. They are acceptable by definition. You don't have to defend them. If you can accept them, even if you don't like them, you have a chance to begin to understand them. This will allow you to move on to the third step, the Spirit, Good Parent, action or Roll step.

### Step Three: Roll!  Making Anger Functional
### "I have power, therefore I will!"

Thanks to the Stop and Drop steps you are no longer lost—but you need to follow some directions to get to where you want to go. The third step, the active Roll step, is getting the appropriate directions and going. This is the step in which your anger is harnessed by your Spirit and used to find the way to soothe your injuries. The challenge here is determining what action you need to take and then having the courage to take it. This is the step in which you get to be a Good Parent to your Hurt Child, completing the cycle and soothing any abandonment feelings still being held by the Hurt Child.

In the second step, you had to learn about your emotional injuries, old and new, and how they were causing you difficulty. You also had to uncover what you were angry about. Remember—anger is energy that is meant to fix what is hurting you, but problems with using anger effectively cause emotional dysfunction.

Anger, as I define it, is a much bigger concept than the way that most people think of it. Most people think of anger as being dangerous and destructive, as yelling and screaming or being violent. But that is the hot end of the anger spectrum. On the cold end of the anger spectrum, anger can be expressed passive-aggressively, by not doing what you've agreed to do. The middle of the spectrum of anger contains what would be considered everyday, assertive behavior. Assertive behavior is based on knowing that your feelings and needs are OK and that it's OK to ask for what you want. If you feel you are not being paid enough at work, for example, the assertive thing to do would be to ask for a raise. Being assertive doesn't guarantee that your needs will be met, but it greatly increases those odds. After all, if you don't ask for the raise, you probably won't get it.

Anger is the source of our personal power. It is meant to empower us in taking care of ourselves. When we act on the world to try to meet our needs, we are using our anger as power. When we act on ourselves to meet our needs, we are being self-nurturing. Both being powerful and self-nurturing are helpful, important, and functional ways to use anger to try to attend to ourselves.

The third step, Roll, is doing what I have just described above. This step is focused on taking the dysfunctional anger, which has been going into problematic thoughts, feelings, or behaviors, and refocusing it on either empowerment or self-nurturing. It's time to start swatting that darned mosquito!

Part of the difficulty of the third step is that how you use your anger for power or nurturing differs from person to person and from situation to situation. It depends on what your Hurt Child needs and what the situation will allow. The use to which you put your anger depends on the nature of your injury and what you subjectively feel would meet your needs. There is not a standard, automatic thing to do with your anger. Each time you work through the third step you are going to have to figure out how to use your anger energy to take care of your Hurt Child. The question that you will need to ask yourself is "What do I need to do with my anger energy that will best take care of me right now?"

## James' Story Concludes

When we left James, he had learned to work the first two steps in the context of his therapy with Sam. Let's take a look at how James learned to make a more effective use of his anger and utilize the action step, the Roll step of the system. This is also the Good Parent or Spirit step.

The situations that caused his explosive anger were ones in which James felt challenged or put down while working. In fact, he lost his job as a result of blowing up at a supervisor who had questioned how James had performed a recent task. When James reviewed this situation with his therapist, Sam, they sorted out what was going on, and why James had such a strong response to the criticism. They successfully connected the situation with his supervisor to James' old injuries, mostly the ones related to his older brother, Steve.

When they looked at what James might have done differently with his anger, at first James could think of nothing positive. Sam pointed out to James that his feelings were very personal information. Since it was personal, his emotions weren't meant to be shared with just anyone, least of all someone he didn't like or trust. James had never thought of his anger as something personal. In fact, he had never thought of his anger in any kind of positive light. He had always been put down for his blowups.

The reality is that sharing your anger with someone is a potential gift. If you tell someone that you are angry with him or her, you are sharing very personal information. It gives that person the chance to deal with the problem. Seen in this context, the anger is an opportunity to improve your relationship. You only want to give that opportunity to someone you think is likely to appreciate the gift and deal with the emotional injury that underlies the anger.

Anger also can be used to hurt or distance others. Sam

pointed out that there were some proper uses for explosive anger, but that it was likely that James only would want to use it in situations where he really needed to defend himself or his family. Those would be situations where he wouldn't care about how the other people might respond to it. Explosive anger is meant to be destructive, and there is a time and place for that kind of behavior.

Holding in anger all the time is part of what causes angry explosions. When anger is dealt with as an appropriate feeling and is used to fix what is causing it, it isn't a problem. When you hold anger in, you are like a pressure cooker with no release valve. You're destined for an explosion as the pressure builds. When you can learn to use your anger effectively in your daily life, it's as if you have a pressure valve that helps you release the pent-up energy.

Sam helped James to see how his outbursts were self-destructive. James came to see that as a result of his explosions he felt worse about both himself and his anger. He also began to see how it set him up for other attacks because people tend to use your vulnerabilities if they want to hurt you. His coworkers, who were frequently competitive with James, also had their own reasons to be angry. They expressed their anger by attacking James. When James would blow up, his coworkers could see a way to get to him. James began to understand that his supervisor, as well as some of his coworkers who used to try to get his goat, really didn't deserve to know that they bothered him.

As Sam and James considered these ideas, they to began to brainstorm about how James could use his anger more effectively. The idea of using anger to build a defense, instead of exploding offensively, began to grow in James' thoughts. As he discussed this idea with Sam, James realized that apart from blowing up, he had never able to defend himself in his relationship with his abusive older brother, Steve.

Sam and James worked on James' ability to recognize his anger earlier. In fact, the goal was for James to be aware of it, on some level, at all times. They agreed that if James felt his anger was acceptable, there were all kinds of things he might be able to do with it to nurture himself. Probably the most important thing would be to conceal his real feelings from the people most likely to trigger his explosions. They worked together on how to build up James' defenses. Part of building up defenses involved taking better care of himself emotionally so that he would be better able to deal with injury. He was also finding new ways to relate to his peers.

Other self-nurturing uses of James' anger included James talking daily with his wife, Alice, about the things that were bothering him at work. James had always protected Alice from these feelings, believing that they were bad. Also, Sam and James discussed James' need to get more individual attention from Alice. They decided that paying for a babysitter once a week, so that James and Alice could have personal time together, was probably a lot less expensive than losing his job or paying a therapist.

Now, you're probably not used to thinking of asking for more time with your spouse or hiring a babysitter as angry behavior. They aren't angry behaviors, but they are a use of the energy of anger. They are powerful behaviors in that they represent an action taken that impacts the world so that you can get your needs met. And power is made out of anger, the natural, healing energy that is meant to fix what is hurting you. Hiring a babysitter and talking to his wife were ways for James to unbend his anger, because part of what was hurting him was lack of attention from his wife. By using his anger appropriately, and turning it into power, he was able to redirect it away from self-destructive, explosive anger, and to use his anger to fix what was causing him pain.

In addition to finding more time with Alice, James and Sam also examined James' life to look for ways to have fun. James had given up a lot of activities when he became a father. But giving up the things that had made him enjoy his life was a here-and-now injury that made him more vulnerable to acting out his anger dysfunctionally.

As James began to work to take better care of himself emotionally, in an ongoing way, he was successful in building up his emotional defenses with his antagonistic coworkers. Interestingly, the work that he had done to better nurture himself had helped to build up his ability to tolerate some smaller emotional injuries. He found that the teasing from some of the guys who liked to give him a hard time at work didn't affect him as much. In fact, as James began to find more fulfillment in his life in general, he noticed that he felt less angry.

James also worked with Sam to come up with specific ways he could redirect his anger with people at work. They discussed strategies meant to discourage criticism of him. They did some role-playing in therapy, practicing how James could learn to smile as a way of holding his boundaries better. They discussed how holding onto a smile could be a way to let the abuser know that he couldn't get to you. James began to practice doing it at his new job and he was astounded at how people responded. Not only did they stop teasing him, they also seemed to like him better. After a while, James could see that some of the times that he had thought people were teasing him, they were actually just joking with him and trying to get to know him better.

James had found yet another way in which his transference had distorted some of his experience. He had become so defensive as a result of the abuse and intimidation he had received in growing up under the domination of his older brother, Steve, that it had damaged the way he related to other men in general. Now, for the first time in his life, James began to become comfortable in friendships with other men. The rock that James had to work so hard to push up the mountain was finally beginning to roll down the other side.

As Sam and James discussed using his anger more effectively, James became aware that he didn't have to respond to a particular upset in a particular way. However, when they did discuss a specific event that was upsetting, James was always able to come up with something he could have done to use his anger more effectively. This process was a way for James to become more and more aware of his options.

Eventually, James was even able to use his emotional defenses to be less vulnerable when he and Alice and the kids got together with the rest of his family at reunions. He still didn't enjoy the time with them, but he could tolerate it for short periods so that his kids could know their grandparents and the extended family.

Like James, as you begin to use your anger to take control of the problems in your life, things will begin to develop a positive momentum. Functional anger replaces the negative momentum of the dysfunctional anger that supports problematic thoughts, feelings, and behaviors. Emotional success breeds more emotional success.

Over time, with practice, you will find that the Stop, Drop, and Roll steps begin to flow into each other naturally. You'll find that you don't have to work quite so hard to know what you're feeling. You'll notice when you're on fire and automatically figure out what's hurting you and attend to the injuries. These will be skills that you have acquired, instead of something that you're working on developing.

This process will be a positive habit that you don't need to think about too much, like brushing your teeth. You'll also find that you'll begin to think psychologically. You'll notice the ability to make sense of your present feelings and understand how they are mixed in with the transference and old injuries. This ability will become second nature as well.

With practice, the third step, the Good Parent, spiritual, Roll step of refocusing your anger into empowerment and self-nurturing, will also become comfortable and natural to you. Like James, you will know how to unbend your anger and use your power to find more fulfillment throughout your life.

# CHAPTER 3

# The Bad Parent, "Good" Kid, and "Bad" Kid

## *The Making of the Hole in Your Heart*

BECAUSE PARENTS ARE HUMAN, THEY ARE VULNERABLE. They can be injured, emotionally or physically. When you're injured—when you're hungry, tired, lonely, thirsty, or sad, for example—you usually function out of your Hurt Child ego state.

When someone is in their Hurt Child state, they are in need of nurturing. Unfortunately, however, when that person is parenting a child while in their Hurt Child ego state, they are reversing the parent-child relationship. Instead of the parent being present to take care of their child, the parent is asking their child to take care of them emotionally. This could happen, for example, when a parent has just gotten home from work and is tired and hungry—but so are the kids and the parent might snap at them when they need to be fed. If the parents have experienced emotional injuries, such as divorce, they may be susceptible to bouts of crying, depression, or explosive anger while the kids are around. Even a parent's own childhood injuries may make them emotionally unavailable to give their kids the care and attention that they need. This type of behavior defines the Bad Parent role, and it is how the hole in your heart was created, regardless of the intensity. And, since we are talking about injuries, remember the emotions that follow: sadness, fear, and anger.

When parents are unable to protect their child from their own emotional injuries, they are functioning as Bad Parents. No one is immune from injury as a parent, and no one is able to protect their child from all of their own emotional injuries. This is why we all experience some amount of Bad Parenting while growing up. When these experiences occur, we all are injured emotionally and receive some level of the Bad Parent voice deposited into our psyches. This voice is characterized by the classic Bad Parent statement: "I'm not here to take care of you; you take care of me!" This Bad Parent voice may be stronger in some of us, due to our inherent genetic makeup (our innate tolerance for injury) and/or the intensity of the Bad Parent messages that we received.

Good Parents are those among us who are aware of the importance of parenting, and who try to be present emotionally for their children whenever they can. There are no perfect parents, however, since everyone is vulnerable to injury while parenting. The best parents among us function as Good Parents the majority of the time. They do their best.

I'd like to stress the fact that there aren't any perfect parents because many people who are trying to heal the hole in their own hearts are functioning as parents at the same time. It is important to not let guilt about the way you have functioned as a parent prevent you from looking at the injuries from your own childhood. It is all too easy for that to happen.

It is a sad fact of life that many parents are so severely damaged that they either don't try very hard to be present for their children's emotional needs or, even worse, actively engage in damaging them. Also, many parents are damaged in ways that they themselves don't understand. These kinds of parents are frequently unaware of the damage that they are passing on to their children. It's usually the case that the greater the amount of damage to the parent, the more injuries the child will receive. This will increase the child's need for psychotherapy.

To help you understand the spectrum of Bad Parenting more specifically, I have come up with seven categories of emotional damage in childhood, which I've listed below. These categories are meant to help you gain a somewhat objective way to understand and validate what may have happened in your process of growing up. They are *not* hard and fast categories. They are only meant to help identify differences in childhood damage and to validate the injuries you may have experienced.

In the categories below, I refer to two terms that I want to clarify. The first is *trauma*, which describes a severe level of an injury, either emotional or physical. Generally, this means having your life threatened or experiencing a severe physical or emotional injury, or watching someone else experience this kind of injury. I believe that almost all emotional injuries are experienced as life threatening, on some level, to young children.

In addressing levels of injury in the categories below, I refer to *severe trauma* as events that are actually life threatening, not those that feel that way. I also discuss *significant trauma*, which are experiences that are seriously abusive, but not life threatening. When I use the term *mild levels of trauma*, I mean that the abuse is mostly emotional in nature. This does not mean that these injuries are not important. They can even be debilitating. Usually, however, they are less so than physical and/or sexual abuse.

In considering sexual abuse, there are many factors that go into determining how destructive these experiences can be. One is the age of the person being abused. Another, again, is the person's innate tolerance for injury. A third is the nature of the relationship of the perpetrator. It is different if it is a parent committing the abuse. A parent's committing sexual abuse with a child is one of the greatest boundary violations and betrayals that a child can experience. A fourth variable is how extensive the abuse is, while a fifth factor to consider is whether the abuse is accompanied by violence. Depending on what the circumstances are, sexual abuse can be a severe to mild level of trauma, but is usually severe to moderate.

Another term I would like to define is *chaos*. Chaos is defined in the dictionary as confusion and disorder. Chaos speaks to the unpredictability of things. When I use this term in the context of abuse, I am referring to the level of disorganization in the family of origin. Children need to have a sense of comfort and stability in their relationships with their parents and to know that they can count on the stability of their environment in a day-to-day way. Constant upheaval in their lives represents another form of injury. In the categories below, there is a higher level of chaos, and therefore also a lower level of stability, in Category One. The level of chaos lessens by degrees as you move from Category One to Category Seven.

I want to emphasize, once again, that different people, each with their own genetic makeup, may have different responses to the same level of emotional damage in their childhoods. Someone who is extremely sensitive may find a childhood with emotional damage just as injurious as someone who was sexually abused. So, please keep these ideas in mind as you review the categories.

## The Seven Categories of Emotional Damage from Childhood

CATEGORY ONE: Parent or parents attempt to murder their child. Severe levels of trauma and chaos are present. There may or may not be sexual abuse.

CATEGORY TWO: Parent or parents threaten to murder their child and/or expose the child to an environment that includes life-threatening behavior (i.e., guns being waived around, knives being thrown) and a high level of emotional chaos. Severe levels of trauma are present, which may or may not include sexual abuse by parents or others.

CATEGORY THREE: The childhood environment has serious levels of chaos and abuse, including sexual abuse. There may or may not be physical and/or emotional abuse. Sexual abuse may be perpetrated by parents or others. Severe levels of trauma are present.

CATEGORY FOUR: The childhood environment has significant levels of chaos and physical and/or emotional abuse, but no sexual abuse by parents. Significant levels of trauma are present.

CATEGORY FIVE: The childhood environment has mild levels of physical and/or emotional abuse, with no or very mild levels of sexual abuse. Significant levels of trauma are present.

CATEGORY SIX: There is an emotionally damaged parent with a significant level of narcissism—the absence of empathy—but no outright abuse. When a parent lacks the ability to empathize with their child, they are much more likely to injure them. Mild levels of trauma may be present with no sexual abuse.

CATEGORY SEVEN: The childhood environment has basically healthy parents who aren't perfect. Mild levels of trauma may be present with no sexual abuse.

In Category Six, I refer to an "emotionally damaged parent with a significant level of narcissism." The parents in categories one through five suffer from emotional damage. When a parent is emotionally damaged, the child will experience them as functioning out of their Hurt Child ego state. Their functioning will include narcissism, as they will have too much injury themselves, frequently, to relate to the injuries that they are causing their children. The impacts of these injuries on the child are greater than the level of damage I am referring to in Category Six, which refers to a milder narcissism.

It is a given that if a parent is involved in direct abuse of their child, regardless of what kind, that parent is suffering from a moderate to severe level of emotional damage. The kinds of problems a damaged parent like this may have can include depression, bipolar disorder, or schizophrenia. This kind of parent may suffer from addictions or anxiety disorders. Even the death of a parent may leave the child feeling neglected or abandoned. All of these kinds of problems are likely to leave a child with the impression of a narcissistic parent.

These categories are meant to help you get some sense of the level of damage and injury that you may have sustained growing up in your family. They are not completely firm. It may not matter a whole lot if you had a Category Six or a Category Seven childhood. The categories are meant to help you put your experience into perspective and relate it to the kinds of problems you may be having in your life as a result of your injuries and the difficulties with anger that follow.

## The Problem of Narcissism

Narcissus is a figure out of Greek mythology, the son of the river Cephissus and the nymph Liriope. (Things like that happen in Greek mythology.) Narcissus was so beautiful that he fell in love with himself when he saw his own image in a pond. Eventually, so entranced with his reflection that he did nothing else but look at it, he wasted away and died.

This last part of the myth is important to keep in mind, since someone suffering from a significant amount of narcissism is vulnerable to the same metaphorical fate. Narcissists end up struggling with their emptiness and isolation if they become aware of these feelings through the contexts of their emotionally intimate relationships. These relationships always suffer, and the individuals suffer as well. The question is will the narcissist notice this and be able to attend to it.

The dictionary defines narcissism as self-love. The Diagnostic and Statistical Manual of Mental Health Disorders characterizes a Narcissistic Personality Disorder partially as a person who displays "a pervasive pattern of grandiosity,...need for admiration and lack of empathy."

Narcissism can be defined in many ways, but the central

issue is not simply the idea that an individual sits around all day looking in the mirror. They don't even have to like the way they look. The real issue is that a narcissist is unable to be empathic with others; the narcissist is unable to imagine what it would be like to feel the emotions and have the experiences of another human being. Narcissists are so caught up in themselves that they don't relate to the needs of others. They end up isolated within themselves even when they're with other people.

In reality, there is a spectrum of narcissism that is part of the human condition. Some level of narcissism is, and needs to be, present in all of us. How much you love yourself and how much you are able to love others is a variable, and we all have different degrees of ability to love ourselves and others. When someone has too little self-love, they are vulnerable to anxiety and depression. At the lowest end, they are at risk for suicide. At the other extreme you find the true sociopaths, people who care so little for others and are so deprived of empathic ability that they are able to use other humans as if they were merely objects. Objects can be manipulated with no sense of remorse, which explains the why the sociopath is comfortable with even the most severely destructive behaviors toward other human beings, including betrayal, theft, rape, and murder.

In its milder forms, problematic narcissism can cause people to be unable to understand each other's emotions. I once talked to a man who was both a father and a husband, and who told me that he wouldn't be talking to me if he hadn't made those life commitments. He told me that, by himself, he was comfortable with avoiding all emotions. I replied that if he hadn't made those commitments in his life he would have become a lonely, bitter old man. Furthermore, I told him, on some level, he'd made those commitments, even if unconsciously, precisely to avoid ending up bitter and alone.

People who suffer from narcissism have underlying injuries. What's important is that, as a result of their injuries, they are frequently unaware of their distancing and withdrawal from the significant others in their lives. They may not seem to suffer from self-love at all. It can look much more like a lack of emotional awareness. This inability to be empathic with their own selves can be another part of what makes dealing with them so difficult. They often don't know or understand what they are feeling and this is what makes narcissists struggle so often with identifying and understanding their own behavior. Frequently, they have no conscious intention of harming those with whom they are emotionally involved.

Narcissism is created in two distinctly opposed and different ways. The first, which is the much more rare method, is the *spoiled child syndrome*. In this context, parents cater to their child's needs and demands in a manner that doesn't require the child to recognize and value the needs of others. When the child reaches his or her "terrible two's" and, as part of the natural developmental process, expects to be in charge of the entire universe, the parents allow the child to be in charge.

The reason this manner of causing narcissism is relatively rare is that life is hard, and there is a lot more injury in the world than overindulgence. In fact, in general, I believe it's better for parents to err on the side of being supportive and nurturing than being overly firm and demanding. As usual, however, finding a healthy balance is important, especially in terms of setting limits for children. They need to have healthy limits, but not ones that are overly intrusive and intense. Those kinds of limits may actually hinder the child's development and self-esteem.

The second way in which narcissism is created is much more common. This method is called the *narcissistic retreat*. The narcissistic retreat is a result of the child's early emotional wounding, when it learns that it just doesn't work to try to meet their needs with another person. The child learns to give up on meeting their emotional needs interpersonally as a result of being unable to connect emotionally with their primary caregivers. This injury can happen in a number of ways. Their Bad Parent could be emotionally unavailable. The child could experience a lack of empathy from their parent. The child may not be seen, valued, and recognized for who he or she is. Parents may not protect their children appropriately. A child may learn that he or she just doesn't count, or that what he or she feels and needs doesn't count. This lesson can cause the child to decide, unconsciously, that it only works to take care of his or her own needs. This child learns not to pursue real love with another person, but instead to turn to things for their central gratification in life. This is why addictions are so pervasive, and why narcissism is related to addiction.

It is important to note that this same dynamic is very much present in people who have adopted a passive-aggressive stance in their relationships, and passive-aggressive behavior is very much a part of addictions as well. People who are narcissistic can lose track of following up on their commitments to other people because they lack the empathic ability to understand how their actions may make the other person feel injured. This kind of behavior is actually an unconscious expression of anger meant for their parents.

When a parent is so injured that they are unable to be empathic with their child and to attend to their child's needs, this piece of narcissism contributes to the Internalized Bad Parent in the child. The more frequently the parent is functioning in their Hurt Child ego state, the more they will demand that their child take care of them. In this manner, the more injured the parent, the more damage is passed on to the child. You will notice that I haven't created a category for perfect parents, since no parent is perfect. Being human, all parents are vulnerable to injury and parenting out of injury. Therefore, no one escapes his or her childhood without some level of damage; it is only a question of how much damage has been sustained.

There is a vicious cycle in which injury causes narcissism in a person who then goes on to have their own children and injure them in a similar fashion with narcissistic behavior. Injury is a central factor in the growth and evolution of civilization

Psychotherapy, then, can be seen as the cutting edge of civilization, as we attempt to heal people one at a time. This book is an attempt to expedite that kind of healing in a broader context than individual psychotherapy.

## "Good" Kids and "Bad" Kids

To children, their parents are giants with the power of life and death over them. This life-and-death aspect of parental power is why I see Post-Traumatic Stress Disorder as the primary underlying diagnosis for everyone in therapy. When your life feels threatened it is traumatic.

Regardless of the intensity of childhood emotional damage, the Bad Parent voice elicits a split in the Hurt Child ego state of the child receiving these messages. The child is in conflict in response to the Bad Parent message. Survival dictates placating or caretaking the Bad Parent, while the anger generated by this injury demands a different response. It is at this critical time that our anger begins to become dysfunctional. This learned dysfunction of anger is functional, in terms of survival in the family. However, it is dysfunctional outside of the family in the world.

The functional angry response of the "Bad" Kid would be one that would demand that the Bad Parent look at the bad parenting, apologize, and change back into Good Parent mode. That would require the Bad Parent to have or develop an awareness of the child's needs and accept them as valid. But typically the Bad Parent doesn't have this awareness, and the Hurt Child splits into being what I call a "Good" Kid and a "Bad" Kid. The effects of this division, and this learned dysfunction of anger, can last long into adulthood.

You may notice the quotation marks around the terms "Good" Kid and "Bad" Kid and you may wonder why they are there. The important and simple reason is that the "Good" Kid isn't really good, and the "Bad" Kid isn't really bad; they each have good and bad traits associated with them. They are only "Good" and "Bad" from the dysfunctional perspective of the Bad Parent.

The "Good" Kid learns to be responsible and to take care of others effectively. In fact, at times I even call this part the Caretaker. Caretaking is good, since it brings many different rewards. Caretakers are great employees and are well respected. However, there is a downside to being a totally "Good" Kid. That downside is being out of touch with one's feelings, which almost always leads to some emotional problems. Those problems would include the relational problems of explosive anger or passive-aggressive anger, depression, anxiety, and addictive behaviors. In addition, "Good" Kids have a tendency toward being workaholics that may be exploited by authority figures in the workplace. They may be well respected and well rewarded, but they may be very unhappy (without realizing it) until they lose their mantle of innocence. The mantle of innocence is the assumption we all make in leaving our families that we're fine in how we function emotionally.

When "Good" Kids first become aware of their unhappiness and lose their mantle of innocence, it's usually in a fitful and halting manner. Frequently they are so committed to denying their emotions that they must experience repeated confrontations to begin to realize the importance of being in touch emotionally. And they are angry, though frequently unconscious of their feelings. Their anger may have been leaching out of them, indirectly in the form of passive-aggressive behavior. Or, when the "Bad" Kid makes its voice heard, it can flare up with explosive anger, depression, or intense anxiety of the kind that George experienced in his panic attack.

The "Bad" Kid is also misunderstood. The "Bad" Kid is bad in that he or she may act out anger or other emotions inappropriately. Sometimes I call this person the Rebel. However, there is an aspect of them that is good, or healthy, because the "Bad" Kid is in touch with his or her emotions. Without their emotional radar—information the "Bad" Kid provides about emotions—the individual is, in effect, flying blind. Emotions are composed of both information and energy. Without these important resources from the "Bad" Kid, an individual is deprived of a great deal of potential personal power. So there are definitely some good things about the "Bad" Kid.

Almost all of us choose a path somewhere on the continuum between the totally "Bad" Kid path of antisocial behavior and the totally "Good" Kid path of selfless sainthood. Now you might think that the correct path is sainthood, but most mental health variables exist on a continuum, or a spectrum, like a rainbow. Most problems in mental health occur when you get too far out on the edges, and most mental health lies in the center of the range of possibilities. This is true of the "Good" Kid/"Bad" Kid spectrum as well. Some people are off to the end of the spectrum, being either the totally "Good" Kid or the totally "Bad" Kid. However, almost all of us have a mix of these two, regardless of which is the dominant aspect in our personality.

The "Good" Kid and "Bad" Kid exist in relation to the Bad Parent, the damaged individual who is parenting out of his or her Hurt Child state. Remember the Bad Parent message: "I'm not going to take care of you. You take care of me." When a giant who has the power of life and death over you says this, it feels life threatening. In order to survive the perceived and/or real threat, the child develops what I call the "Good" Kid Voice. The "Good" Kid is in charge of placating the Bad Parent, and therefore, surviving. In order to accomplish this, the "Good" Kid part of us represses the difficult, resentful feelings that the child naturally experiences in response to the Bad Parent message. These repressed feelings are the material from which the "Bad" Kid Voice is born. The "Bad" Kid part of us is filled with all kinds of emotions, including, but not limited to, the negative emotions such as anger, sadness, envy, jealousy, and fear.

The narcissism of the Bad Parent injures the child by causing the "Good" Kid/"Bad" Kid split. This split causes the child to struggle to be in touch emotionally and to be able to use the information and energy of its anger to address injuries through all aspects of its life. The child has been trained to be compliant and hide his emotions from himself and others and be a caretaker, or he has chosen to be more of a rebel, and suffer the injuries of being a "problem child." Both stances represent alternative ways of coping with the injury of Bad Parenting.

Neither role is a healthy response by itself. The problem, then, is one of discovering these aspects of one's self and finding a way to begin to unbend the anger for the Bad Parent and turn it into empowerment. Getting the anger away from an internal struggle between "Good" Kid and "Bad" Kid frees it up to address the injury from the Bad Parent.

## Ellen's Story

Ellen was a fifty-three-year-old woman who suffered from a moderate level of major depression. She was isolated and emotionally unavailable to herself and others. Ellen's husband had divorced her more than twenty years ago and her children had grown up and moved far away from her. She didn't know how to make a new life for herself and had withdrawn from most social interaction.

When Ellen was twelve, her mother, Louise, had died of cancer after being ill for almost two years. Raised in Chicago, Ellen was an only child who was close to her mother. Her father, Mike, was a traveling salesman who sold women's clothing to department stores throughout the Midwest. Mike was away frequently and emotionally distant from Ellen when he was home. Mike and Louise had a close and loving relationship, but Mike just didn't know much about how to relate to kids, and especially to a daughter.

When Louise first became ill, Ellen noticed that her parents were upset, but really didn't understand what was going on. Her father seemed more irritable with her, and her mother just seemed more afraid and distracted. Finally, after her mother's first hospital stay, she told Ellen about her illness. As Louise continued to deteriorate, Mike took his daughter aside and told her how she'd have to take care of her mother when he was out of town. Ellen was already a "Good" Kid, but her upcoming life injuries were going to intensify that position. She and her mother got along really well, and

Ellen was invested in doing things right.

As Louise got worse and worse, Mike retreated further and further into himself emotionally. Ellen had never been all that out-going to begin with and she began to withdraw from her friends in order to take care of her mother. Ellen also felt different from her friends, since none of them had to deal with a sick parent. Feeling different at this stage of life was hard on her self-esteem.

During this period of physical and emotional development, Ellen needed her father's support to be valued as a person and not viewed just as a sex object. Her mother helped Ellen to deal with the onset of puberty and menstruation, but Louise's health was failing and she didn't have the energy to explain much more than the basics. Mike, who had never been all that emotionally available, buried his grief in his work and, as a result, was even less present for Ellen.

Mike wasn't obviously narcissistic in his basic personality type. He wasn't focused on himself. He was emotionally connect-ed to his wife and to his close friends. Yet, in his grief, he was unavailable to Ellen. Though she couldn't have articulated it, to her he was narcissistic. To her, he was so lost in his own pain that he just wasn't there for her emotionally. She was such a "Good" Kid, of course, that she never complained. She knew, without it being spo-ken, that she was not supposed to complain.

Mike was functioning in his Hurt Child ego state whenever he wasn't working. He had nothing left to give to Ellen. He didn't know how to deal with his own emotions, let alone deal with Ellen's emotional needs. This left Mike feeling inadequate. He withdrew even further when there was any indication that Ellen was upset.

Ellen's injury of the loss of her mother and her feelings of abandonment left her depressed. The continued and escalating emo-tional abandonment of her father only served to make things worse. She wasn't depressed in an obvious way. She didn't become anorexic or suicidal. She just went into a sad and lonely place that left others at a distance.

But Ellen was truly a "Good" Kid. She still worked hard in

school and earned good grades. She worked after school and saved her money. She cooked for herself and for her father when he was in town. Now, she could have chosen the "Bad" Kid path and become rebellious and promiscuous, since, after her mother's death, she was more or less unsupervised. However, since she had already chosen the "Good" Kid path, and wasn't allowed to know her own feelings, her anger turned inwards into depression and isolation.

Later, when Ellen began to date, she found herself attracted to men who were emotionally unavailable. When she found her husband, Daniel, he was somewhat emotionally unavailable. Ellen was always insecure about herself and her role in the marriage. She did a good job of loving and raising the children, even though parts of her remained sad and unavailable. However, her husband, Daniel, was pretty disconnected from the kids—in much the same way that Ellen's father, Mike, had been. She was always afraid that Daniel would leave her, so she attempted to avoid any confrontation or conflict with him.

When Daniel divorced Ellen, her self-esteem was in the tank. It never had been all that good, even when she was growing up. She had been introverted by nature, and her abandonment by her mother and father left her with even lower self-esteem. During the course of her marriage, she had become increasingly insecure about herself and her interactions with people.

After her kids grew up and left home, she continued to withdraw. One day, however, Ellen found herself walking around her house in tears for the whole day. She had never gotten dressed. The painful loneliness, long contained in her "Bad" Kid, finally broke through the barriers her "Good" Kid had defended for so long. Ellen began to realize that she didn't want to spend the rest of her life so alone. She needed some help and eventually decided to try some counseling.

Ellen had internalized parent figures that were abandoning in general, and who demanded that she take care of them. She had received basic love, warmth, and caring from her mother, Louise;

however, Louise had abandoned her in death the way that her father, Mike, abandoned Ellen both emotionally and physically. Neither of her parents had meant to harm her. However, without speaking the words, her father had told her not to need anything from him. Her mother had done the same, without intending to do so. Louise had simply withdrawn as her cancer drained her energy and, in effect, asked Ellen not to need anything. In addition to these indirect communications, Ellen received similar direct messages, such as when Louise asked Ellen, over and over again, to physically care for her. Mike had also asked directly, many times, for Ellen to help out by caretaking his wife.

Even though her parents had no intention of hurting her, Ellen ended up experiencing a Category Five childhood, in which there was mild abuse in the form of neglect and a significant trauma in the loss of her mother. Her mother's death and neediness had injured Ellen the same way that narcissism injures. Her father's withdrawal into his own injuries had its narcissistic impact, too.

In response, Ellen learned to be the "Good" Kid and take care of her parents' emotional needs. The anger she had stored up in her repressed "Bad" Kid went into depression and low self-esteem.

## Understanding Ellen's Story

Let's look at Ellen's "Good" Kid/"Bad" Kid dynamics. Ellen was a seriously "Good" Kid in terms of her life stance. She didn't rebel when she was asked—or commanded—to become the caretaker for her sick mother. She didn't rebel when her father continued to work and travel after her mother died, thereby asking her non-verbally not to need any attention. He expected her to continue to take care of their apartment. He expected her to clean. He expected her to cook both for herself and for him when he returned home. She was expected not to need anything other than a roof over her head and his financial support.

Ellen responded the way "Good" Kids do. If the parent

says "Jump," the "Good" Kid responds with "How high?" When I said this to one client, he told me that his alcoholic parents would drag him out of bed to entertain their guests at their drunken parties and tell him to jump—and he would have to respond by asking "How high?"

This learned behavior comes at a price: the child learns to ignore his or her emotions. The child learns to enter into relationships with his or her total focus on taking care of the other person while ignoring his or her own needs. This sets up the "Good" Kid to be taken advantage of by narcissists or even just by assertive people.

Ellen, of course, also had the specific transference dynamics resonating with her father's emotionally distant and abandoning ways. This led her to find her husband, Daniel, who was looking for a full-time caretaker. He wanted a family, but didn't want to give up anything. Given her low self-esteem and anxiety issues, Ellen was only too happy to avoid the world of work and the competition and criticisms that might have awaited her there.

Women, in general, are especially vulnerable to being overly caretaking of others. There are cultural expectations for women to be caretakers, and women are also biologically programmed to nurture others. They are provided with breasts to feed and nurture children, and their hormonal systems support these nurturing processes.

Caretaking is a valuable skill. Life could not continue without it. However, our society frequently seems to deny this by not paying well those who are in the major caretaking professions: childcare and teaching. With the advent of managed care, we are seeing the devaluation of the medical field as well.

Our society does reward, however, "Good" Kid caretaking behavior in the context of work. "Good" Kids are overly responsible and can be seduced into workaholic behavior. Part of what makes work so addicting to "Good" Kids is that they can be rewarded (at last!) for taking care of everything and attending to all of the details.

On the other hand, totally "Bad" Kids have a hard time making it. They usually are vulnerable to alcoholism, drug abuse, criminality, prostitution, and other forms of dysfunctional angry behavior. They get in trouble with their parents, the law, their partners, and almost every authority figure. It's hard for them to hold a job, and they are often seen as difficult people. They also become aware of losing their mantle of innocence painfully, usually through what Alcoholics Anonymous calls *hitting bottom*. Bottom is the point at which they become so tired of the pain that they cause themselves and others that the alternative of inspecting their lives and problems becomes more attractive than continuing their misery.

Typically, "Good" Kids repress the "Bad" Kids so that they may protect the Bad Parent from their anger. Remember, anger is energy as well as information, and the energy of anger has to go somewhere. When "Good" Kids win the struggle and repress their anger, it goes into dysfunction. In Ellen's case, it turned into a major depression. Ellen's "Good" Kid won the struggle, yet her "Bad" Kid was able to gain her attention by causing her to be depressed. In some ways, the "Good" Kid/"Bad" Kid struggle is like marriage counseling in that both sides have to win to create a success.

### Bringing the "Good" and "Bad" Kids Together

Most of us lie in the middle of the spectrum of "Good" Kid/"Bad" Kid behavior, even if one side does predominate. We also painfully lose our mantle of innocence. In order to begin to make some transition in our identity, and begin to really grow up and make our anger functional, we must have the power to confront the internalized Bad Parent voice. In order to reach empowerment, we have to begin to bring our distant and alienated "Kids" into some kind of alliance.

This is not an easy task. It really can look like marriage counseling at times, with the two "Kids" bickering (and worse) with each other. Role-playing with these two parts in therapy is helpful, as the client gets to externalize an internal conflict. When a conflict is internalized, it often feels the same way that a dog chasing its tail looks—lots of dust gets stirred up, but there's no progress. When the conflict becomes externalized, issues have a chance to become clarified, and, over time, resolved.

Most people will find that they must have a series of conversations between their "Good" Kid and their "Bad" Kid before they begin to see a transition in the relationship. The messages that they've received from their Bad Parent have been powerfully locked in, and it takes a great deal of faith and courage to confront them. Below is a version of a diagram that I created in 1979, after about three years of practice.

Figure 1 is graphic representation of some of the internalized dynamics that operate and can be problematic in all of us. The process of healing these internal relationships is discussed in Chapter Eight.

As you look at this diagram, you can see that as a result of the communication barriers, the "Bad" Kid is stuck with the anger it feels. If the anger gets directed toward the Bad Parent, the "Good" Kid intervenes and cuts it off. The anger of the "Bad" Kid may get directed at the "Good" Kid, or the "Good" Kid may reflect it back against the "Bad" Kid. Either way, the anger that is meant for the Bad Parent

## Dynamics of Dysfunction

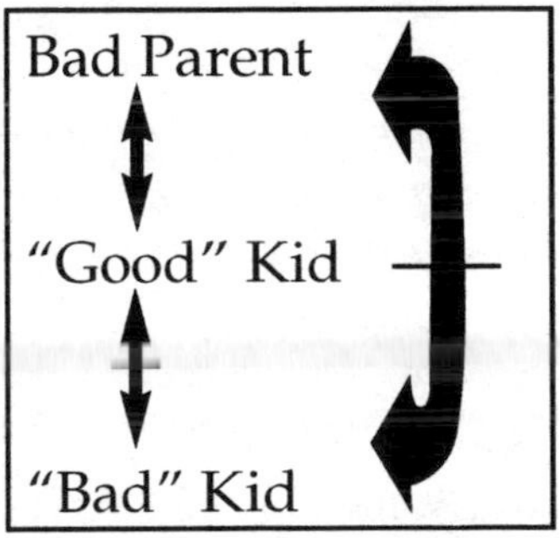

*Figure 1:* *The "Good" Kid is loved, yet not in touch with feelings. The "Bad" Kid is rejected, hurt, angry, and in touch with feelings. The arrows represent lines of communication, which are barred if communication is difficult.*

doesn't get delivered and goes into some form of dysfunction. That dysfunction may be depression, anxiety, drug and alcohol abuse, or extramarital affairs. Whatever form it takes, it will result in problems.

In Ellen's case, her "Good" Kid was in complete charge of her life. Like Ellen, many extreme "Good" Kids will experience what I call a *demand quality* to relationships. This means that, in any relationship, instead of being able to consider the question "When does it take care of me to take care of you?," the extreme "Good" Kid has only one choice. The choice is always to take care of the other.

Many of these extreme "Good" Kids tend to withdraw from as many relationships as possible. It is only with their selves that they are able to be taken care of. They experience the demand quality of relationship, frequently unconsciously, almost as if it were an irresistible undertow. They drown in it or retreat.

Besides becoming isolated, Ellen was stuck with her anger, as her "Good" Kid barred her from using it against her Bad Parent, or almost anywhere else in her life. It is no surprise, then, that her anger cycled back against herself in the form of depression and low self-esteem. She would say terribly angry things to herself about her worth and value, anger she would never express to anyone else, even if it were warranted.

There are times in therapy when the therapist needs to align with the "Good" Kid. Examples of this would be when a client is anti-social or overwhelmed by emotions. Most frequently, however, the therapist aligns with the "Bad" Kid. Since one of the roles of the "Good" Kid is to protect the Bad Parent from the "Bad" Kid, the "Bad" Kid is usually outnumbered. The alignment of the therapist helps to even the sides somewhat.

## "Good" Kid Backlash

When people begin to make changes in therapy, it is, by definition, an unsettling experience. People begin to redefine themselves. Clients frequently experience some level of what I call "Good" Kid Backlash. This phenomenon describes situations where the client makes a move toward changing the emotional status quo by becoming more assertive and empowered and also validating the emotions of the "Bad" Kid. A client may have an unusually effective session, or role-play, and leave the office on a high note. Later, they may experience an upsurge in anxiety or greater depression. It often looks and feels like two steps forward and three steps back.

When Ellen finally got into therapy for her depression, she chose a woman, since she got most of her nurturing from her mother. Dr. Martha Reilly was a psychiatrist who had been trained in Gestalt therapy, which frequently uses role-playing as a technique to facilitate contact with emotions. Dr. Reilly worked with Ellen to be more assertive and encouraged her to try some role-playing to access more of her anger, although it was quite a while before Ellen was ready to try it. Ellen also began taking an antidepressant medication, which helped lighten her mood after a few months.

After Ellen had become accustomed to role-playing, Dr. Reilly encouraged her to try a session working with her mother and her tremendous feelings of loss. It was an emotional session, with lots of tears.

A month later, Dr. Reilly suggested Ellen try to work into her anger with her father. It took two more sessions for Ellen to take the plunge and get angry with her father while role-playing. That evening, Ellen got really depressed. She felt suicidal for the first time in her life. Ellen assumed it would lighten up the next day, but it didn't. She called Dr. Reilly and scheduled an emergency session. Dr. Reilly explained that Ellen was experiencing "Good" Kid Backlash. While it didn't make the increased symptoms of depression disappear overnight, Ellen was relieved to know the reason for her downswing.

Dr. Reilly increased Ellen's antidepressant medication, and they focused more on Ellen's working into her anger with her father. As Ellen became accustomed to working with her anger, her mood improved dramatically over the next few months.

For most clients, this backlash process is one that continues with a relatively quick recovery. There may be further setbacks, but fairly rapidly, over the next few weeks of therapy, the backlash recedes and vanishes. The client experiences less and less discomfort, while at the same time begins to reap the benefits of unbending his or her anger into increased empowerment.

However, for some clients, "Good" Kid Backlash becomes a major impediment to treatment. This is especially true in cases where there has been serious traumatic emotional injury. When this happens, it's time to pay special attention to the concept of the *therapeutic window*.

John Briere, a well-known and respected psychologist researcher on trauma at UCLA, has put forth the concept of the therapeutic window in treating Post-Traumatic Stress Disorder (PTSD). Briere uses the idea of a therapeutic window, a concept from psychiatry, as a metaphor in psychotherapy. In psychiatry, the term refers to finding the appropriate level of antidepressant medication in the blood. If you have too little medication, it has no effect. If you have too much antidepressant in the blood, it will not cross the blood-brain barrier, and, again, has no effect. But within the therapeutic window, the medication becomes effective.

Briere uses an analogy between the medication therapeutic window and the way clients work in therapy when re-experiencing the emotional aspects of trauma. Part of recovering from emotional injuries involves allowing the body to process emotions that were put on hold at the time of the trauma in order to survive. As with medication, entirely avoiding those emotions will not help the recovery. However, it is important to revisit these emotions without having them become re-traumatizing. If the client is re-traumatized, the therapeutic benefit disappears.

The goal is to access and process the emotions in the here and now, without being emotionally overwhelmed. It isn't unusual for clients, at times, to feel overwhelmed emotionally during the process, and when this happens it doesn't always cause further damage. In fact, this intense re-experiencing happens often enough that it has a name—*catharsis*. The trick is to have some catharsis without being re-traumatized. That is why we attempt to stay within the therapeutic window.

Working through or re-experiencing the emotions attached to old injuries is done to help the client, in the here and now, come to terms with all of the emotions involved in the injuries that took place in the there and then. The range of emotions that can be accessed in this process includes sadness, fear, pain, and anger.

The "Bad" Kid's anger is important in the recovery process, since it's used to confront the "Good" Kid and the Bad Parent. The "Bad" Kid, with help from the aligned therapist, uses the anger to break the alliance between the "Good" Kid and the Bad Parent, develop a new alliance with the "Good" Kid, and eventually confront the Bad Parent, eliciting change.

## The Case of Walter

To clarify how the concepts of "Good" Kid Backlash and the therapeutic window manifest in someone's life, let's take a look at Walter. Walter was a twenty-nine-year-old man from Oregon. Walter grew up in a Catholic family, the fifth of eight children. His parents, Betty and Frank, were uneducated, poor, and hard working. Frank worked as a lumberjack when he was younger, but eventually progressed to having a supervisory job in the mill. Betty stayed at their rural home and took care of the kids.

Both Betty and Frank were devoutly religious and took the kids to church every Sunday. The children certainly roughhoused a lot, especially the boys, but all of their kids were pretty good kids. Betty was pretty demanding of them. She hoped that at least one of the sons would become a priest and she encouraged them to become altar boys. Frank was religious too, but not as interested in having his sons go into the priesthood.

When Walter was seven, a new priest came to their church; Father Donald had been transferred from a larger diocese in Chicago. Father Donald was quite charming, and everyone in the church quickly developed a great deal of respect and affection for him. The only problem was that, unbeknownst to the congregation, Father Donald was a pedophile who preyed on young boys. He had gotten into trouble in Chicago, and was transferred to rural Oregon to avoid a scandal.

Father Donald struggled with his perverse desires. He became a priest to avoid his issues with sexuality. However, those feelings, like all feelings, don't just disappear because they are uncomfortable. His unacceptable angry sexual feelings continued to press him.

Walter was an attractive young boy but vulnerable as a result of the lack of attention available in his busy family. Eventually he became the focus of the priest's fantasies and desires. Father Donald bestowed a great deal of attention on Walter. The priest talked to Walter's parents and let them know that he saw a great deal of ability in Walter. He told them that he thought that Walter had both the intelligence and spirituality to become a priest some day, if he had the proper development.

Over time, Father Donald offered Walter scholarships for camping trips with some of the other boys, as well as visits to other churches so that he could get a broader picture of the church and the world. Betty was especially thrilled to think that Walter might become the priest she had hoped for. Frank and Betty had no idea that Father Donald was slowly seducing their son.

It took Father Donald almost two years to begin sexual activity with Walter. Their relationship had become very close emotionally before the priest introduced any sexual contact. By that time, Walter trusted Father Donald implicitly. When the priest told him that these behaviors were an extension of their closeness and an appropriate way for expressing reverence for God, Walter believed him. Father Donald made sure that Walter knew that this was to be their secret. In this way, he put on Walter the burden of protecting Father Donald from harm.

As Walter approached his teenage years, his parents began to notice that his behavior changed. Sometimes Walter seemed dispirited and listless, while at other times he had angry outbursts. Frank and Betty ascribed this to hormones and normal teenage stuff, but as time went on, Walter didn't seem to improve. Eventually, he began to back away from his involvement with the church. When his parents questioned him about what he was doing, he eventually, reluctantly, told them what had been going on.

Walter was both scared and embarrassed to tell them. As mad as he was at Father Donald, he still cared about him and felt a need to protect him. He was also afraid that the information about his relationship with Father Donald would come out and that the other kids at school would find out.

Frank and Betty didn't know what to do. They loved the church and were committed to their religion, but they knew that what had gone on was terribly wrong. Yet, at the same time, they felt that they needed to protect their son.

Eventually, they decided to back away from their parish and attend another church in a town much farther away. They let Father Donald understand that they knew what had gone on and told him that they would be watching him. They felt it would be too difficult and disturbing to Walter if they openly confronted all of the issues in the context of their little town and parish.

While Walter was relieved by his parents' involvement, he didn't recover all that quickly. He certainly wasn't interested in going to church anymore. Betty and Frank understood this and didn't push him to attend with them, though it still bothered Betty a great deal. Gradually, Walter started to become more outgoing with his friends, but he never seemed to be quite as comfortable and close with them as he had been in the past. His grades in school recovered quite quickly, but his angry outbursts at home, triggered by his underlying resentment about not having been protected from the abuse, continued for years.

Walter eventually left home and put himself through college. He was a hard worker and quite bright. He met his wife, Amy, at the University of Oregon, and they married shortly after they graduated and moved to a small city in Oregon. Walter got a job as a librarian and Amy worked as a clerk in the city government. Amy and Walter were both quiet and thoughtful people, and they lived comfortably and happily for a number of years.

Walter came in for treatment shortly after the birth of their first son, Brian. He had become seriously depressed and couldn't understand why. Amy convinced him to talk to his family doctor, Josephine Carrington. Dr. Carrington put Walter on an antidepressant medication. When Walter didn't seem to improve as rapidly as both he and Dr. Carrington would have liked, the doctor referred him to a psychologist, Dr. Knudsen.

Walter began to sort out his problems with Dr. Knudsen. They were able to connect his sexual abuse to the many ways that it had affected him. As they worked together, Walter began to see the role that his anger at Father Donald had played in his depression. He had not known that he was angry, but was confused about what was the right thing to do. Walter's "Good" Kid had wanted to take care of his parents and be a good Catholic boy, and also to please Father Donald. Since angry energy has to go somewhere, Walter had turned it against himself, telling himself that it was his fault. He also looked at the ways in which that anger had joined with his fears to lead him into a significantly isolated lifestyle. Walter was experiencing the demand quality of "Good" Kids in relationships. His default mode of relating was to take care of others, regardless of his needs. Since this kind of behavior had brought him so much pain, it seemed easier to keep a distance from others. It reduced both his fear and his pain, yet it left him isolated.

Dr. Knudsen encouraged him to validate and accept his angry feelings in the context of his therapy. They tried some role-playing exercises and she began to encourage Walter to express his anger out loud.

As Walter did some of these exercises, he felt elated at first. It was incredibly freeing to yell at Father Donald about all the pain of betrayal and shame. Unfortunately, after the session was over and

Walter returned to the comfort of his home, he experienced a major panic attack. Walter paged Dr. Knudsen, and, when she called him back, she was able to help him put things in perspective and calm down. She also talked the next day with Dr. Carrington about obtaining anti-anxiety medication for Walter in case this situation arose again.

In their next session, Dr. Knudsen discussed the dynamic of the "Good" Kid Backlash. She explained how, sometimes, when you make some forward movement in therapy and it upsets the status quo, it can feel very threatening to the "Good" Kid. The "Good" Kid, when threatened, can strike back and try to intimidate the "Bad" Kid. In reality, this is an attempt to get the system to return to the old, dysfunctional ways of coping. Even though the old ways of coping had led to Walter's depression, it still felt more comfortable to the "Good" Kid than to allow all of these strong emotions to be expressed. They had been repressed for so long that it was disorienting to let them surface.

As they continued to sort out and make sense of what was happening, they looked at how strongly Walter's "Good" Kid had been conditioned. They looked at how his parents had been strong believers in the church's views of good and evil, as well as the concept of sin. These beliefs, as well as his family's and church's strictness, had impacted Walter powerfully. Even though he had distanced himself from the church while he was quite young, he was still strongly conditioned to act out the "Good" Kid role in his life.

In spite of Walter's high level of intellectual ability, he would kind of freeze up during sessions. This could happen by just beginning to look at and discuss the issues of his sexual abuse and his experience with the church. It would happen even after Walter had talked many times about the abuse. It happened frequently after he accessed his angry feelings, too. Walter and Dr. Knudsen discussed this dynamic, and again attributed this to "Good" Kid Backlash. Walter's "Good" Kid would literally shut down his cognitive functioning at times. The "Good" Kid would also quickly change his anger into fear.

Luckily, Dr. Knudsen had seen this type of reaction before and reassured Walter that these reactions were a function of his anxiety and related to his primary diagnosis of Post-Traumatic Stress Disorder. The injury of his sexual abuse by Father Donald, and the resulting fears he developed about trusting people in general, had led to his isolated lifestyle.

As Dr. Knudsen discussed the impact of these injuries, it became clear to them that Walter's major depression surfaced as a result of the birth of his son, Brian. Walter wasn't aware of how his old feelings of anger, shame, and fear were brought back by his son's arrival. He wasn't aware of his fears and anxieties about having his son exposed to a world where Brian might become injured in a similar way. The fact that Walter, as the "Good" Kid, didn't know he was having these feelings only made him more vulnerable. The anger that accompanied the fears and pain had been fueling his depression and feelings of helplessness.

Dr. Knudsen and Walter worked to moderate the amount of anxiety that he experienced in sessions. "Good" Kid Backlash continued to be a major impediment to treatment, but over time it receded. Partly this related to his medication regime. It was also due, in part, to Walter coming to trust Dr. Knudsen. As their relationship continued, Walter felt secure in her competence and caring. Her explanations of feelings and experiences that had been quite disturbing and upsetting for Walter helped tremendously in this process. Part of the value of their relationship, which they also discussed, was the transference dynamic between Dr. Knudsen and Walter's mother. Dr. Knudsen was both warm and accepting of Walter. This helped his transition into a place where he could be more accepting of his "Bad" Kid. Dr. Knudsen's support and caring, along with her giving him permission to have his feelings, helped to reduce the impact that Walter's mother's strict and demanding nature had had on him while growing up.

Hopefully, as you have read through this chapter, you have

begun to get a clear understanding of what Bad Parenting is all about, as well as the way in which it elicits the internal split in all of us. Healing the "Good" Kid/"Bad" Kid split is a significant piece of the overall healing process, and the anger that was caused by the initial injuries, as well as the more recent ones, will play a central role in taking back power for recovery.

# CHAPTER 4

# Anger and Anxiety

## *"Fear Is the Mind Killer"*

EARLY IN FRANK HERBERT'S WONDERFUL SCI-FI NOVEL *Dune*, the quote "Fear is the mind killer" appears as an insight into character development. I think this is a concise and powerful understanding of the impact of anxiety. I often tell my clients that anxiety will take away everything that you let it take—including one's mind. It's interesting, if not ironic, that those who undertake psychotherapy to heal from anxiety both need and have tremendous courage, because it takes courage to face one's fears, even though that courage may feel like desperation to those in pain.

As I've already explained, beyond genetics, I believe most problems in mental health are based on problems we have in dealing with our anger. Again, I define anger as the natural energy that the body generates to fix or heal injury. But anger is only one response to injury. One can also feel sadness, which is the grieving of the injury. One can feel fear, too, which is the desire to not be hurt again. And, fear, like anger, carries a lot of energy. The energy of fear is meant to avoid being hurt again.

Anxiety goes one step further. With anxiety, we are dealing with the interface of two of the secondary emotions to injury, fear and anger. Anger can seem fairly simple in comparison to fear. Anger is the energy in response to an injury. Fear and anger are closely related, since both are triggered by injury, and both are kinds of energy the body produces. In fear the energy is for flight, or avoiding further injury. In anger, the energy is for fight, or to fix what is hurting you. They can combine when one is experiencing injury and threat simultaneously. In situations like that, the person being injured and threatened has anger, but it's unsafe to show it. Showing it would only result in further injury. Therefore, the angry energy can only join with the fear already present. This produces anxiety, or fear exaggerated by the energy of anger.

Fear, which has always been very useful in survival, is about trying to avoid future injury. Since people can be injured in so many possible ways, people often have difficulty sorting out realistic fears from non-realistic (neurotic) fears. Neurotic fears are a form of anxiety and occur when the unexpressed and contained anger energy flows into and exaggerates fears.

The most concise way to make clear the difference between fear and anxiety is the following metaphor. When a bear is chasing you in the woods, you feel fear. Anxiety is when there is no bear but you still feel like a bear is chasing you.

One of the problems with anxiety is that you feel that it's completely out of your control, like the weather. It is something that happens to you, and, like rain, you can prepare for it, but cannot control it. You can bring an umbrella, but you still have to accept the fact that it is raining.

This leaves you with the question of how to deal with it. The problem with only learning how to deal with anxiety is that you continue to suffer from it. It doesn't solve the problem. In treating anxiety, you are faced with three main problems. The first is that you need to stop the intense pain of anxiety from continuing to traumatize you. Once this is accomplished, you need to understand what the anxiety is all about. You must figure out why it's there. And, finally, you need to take back the energy of anger and use it to put your fear into an appropriate perspective.

In the following sections, I'll explain how to put these three steps into action to eliminate the problems caused by your anxiety.

## Step One: Controlling Your Anxiety

The first step in treating your anxiety is to learn ways to control it. This isn't easy. One reason why anxiety is so difficult to cope with is that the most intense levels of anxiety—panic attacks as well as intense anxiety attacks—are the most painful of human experiences. In fact, intense anxiety can far surpass most physical pain. This can make anxiety a traumatizing experience.

Once we have been traumatized by anxiety, the normal fears of life can have much greater impact. When this happens, we are much more vulnerable to escalation. *Escalation* is when you begin to experience any level of anxiety, which is a normal part of daily life, as a trigger for more anxiety. When this begins to happen, anxiety can spiral out of control and cause a panic or anxiety attack. We become afraid that we'll become even more afraid. You can see how insidious this cycle can become, and why the escalation can be so rapid.

In treating anxiety, as in treating any emotional problem, you try everything and see what works for you. There are many ways to control anxiety, and it is very important that you find at least one option that works for you. You need to understand that anxiety problems do not need to continue. It is important for you to find, in short order, a way to stop the pain and regain control.

I often use the metaphor of skiing to help people understand anxiety. When skiing, people are afraid of looking downhill because when you ski, you tend to go in the direction that you are looking. If you look downhill and keep going downhill, you'll go faster and faster until eventually you'll get out of control. If you don't stop, you'll hit a tree, or something else, and get seriously hurt or die. This is a realistic fear. But skiers learn to use the edges of their skis to keep in control, and when they're in control, they are not afraid.

Just like skiers use the edges of their skis, when facing the frequently undefined fears of anxiety, we need ways to be in control. This can mean a number of possible approaches.

I believe that relaxation is the best thing available to regain control, since humans can't be both relaxed and anxious at the same time. If you aren't suffering too severely, you may want to learn self-hypnosis or another relaxation technique such as biofeedback, meditation, deep breathing, or the Jacobsen technique. The Jacobsen technique involves lying down and tensing the muscles in your body using isometrics. For example, you can tense your arm by pulling your hand toward you and pushing it away simultaneously. You tense one muscle group of you body at a time, and when you relax it, focus on the feeling of relaxation. As you work through your entire body, you become relaxed.

Clients can use psychotherapists of various backgrounds to learn these techniques, and many relaxation audiotapes are available as well. I also recommend the normal things that you might already use to relax: taking a bath, exercising, or listening to music.

Once you've learned how to go to that place of deep relaxation, you can use that skill to intervene in an anxiety process. One of the best techniques for combating anxiety is my Stop, Drop, and Roll technique.

The first step in that process, Stop, is to notice the anxiety before it becomes overwhelming, and then take a time out. The second step, Drop, would be to stop and look thoughtfully at what is causing those feelings to surface. To help this process, you can ask the following questions:

- What's making me feel fear right now?
- What am I feeling angry about right now?
- What's hurting me right now?
- What's the old business from my past that this relates to?

Roll, the final step, is to utilize a relaxation technique that you have already learned or to engage in some behavior that uses the anger to address the current or old injuries in some manner.

Another important way to cease being traumatized by anxiety is to use prescription medications. My experience is that most people don't like to rely on medication. However, if you are suffering intensely, a small amount of tranquilizers, prescribed by either a family doctor or a psychiatrist, can be an immense help. It is important to understand that these are potentially addictive medications. They relieve anxiety, but when they wear off there can be an initial period of increased anxiety. After relaxing and avoiding the escalation of anxiety, most people can tolerate the brief period of raised anxiety. My experience is that most anxiety clients are afraid of addiction and treat these medications with the respect that they deserve and do not abuse them.

If you decide that you would benefit from a tranquilizer, you will need to go to a medical doctor for a prescription. You will need to understand, experientially, how these medications will work for you. Discuss this with your doctor before you fill the prescription. I recommend that when you get your small supply and are not in a state of anxiety, you take one half of a dose, one to two hours after eating, at home in the evening. This will allow you to understand the way the medication affects you before you take it in a social or work context.

There are also antidepressant medications for those who also experience depression or whose anxiety is stubborn or resistant to short-term interventions. These medications are not addictive, but take longer to work for many people. Some clients take tranquilizers to start treatment either while they are waiting for their antidepressants to begin to work or if they want to put off taking antidepressants until they are sure they need them. In situations where the anxiety is more resistant, clients may take both.

I refer clients to psychiatrists for medication when possible or necessary. Psychiatrists are medical doctors who specialize in treating mental health problems, and so, in general, are more informed and aware of how to use the appropriate (they're called *psychotropic*, meaning that they affect the psyche) medications. A good psychiatrist is necessary in more complicated and difficult cases. However, for relatively mild and uncomplicated situations, I do not hesitate to enlist a client's primary care physician. They tend to be less expensive and more available than psychiatrists, who are in tremendous demand.

By the way, it's important to note that alcohol, while it will reduce anxiety temporarily, is not the medication of choice. Alcohol is more readily available than tranquilizers and also addictive. More importantly, alcohol is a depressant. It acts initially as a stimulant on the nervous system and then it rapidly becomes a depressant. People who suffer from anxiety frequently either also suffer from depression or are vulnerable to doing so. Anxiety and depression are cousins, if you will. They are closely related, and self-medicating with alcohol can have serious and/or disastrous consequences.

## Step Two: Understanding Your Anxiety

Once you have found a way to control your anxiety, the next step is to begin to understand why you have been suffering from it. Many people who have been suffering from anxiety feel that once it is gone, their problems are over. But the anxiety was there for a reason. Anxiety problems may be the loss of innocence that is meant to launch your self-discovery process. It's a way for you to tell yourself that something is really bothering you—and you need to find out what it is.

Certainly there are genetic issues that can be related to anxiety. Some people are born with a greater level of sensitivity than others. Sensitivity, like other abilities such as intelligence or athletic ability, can work for you or against you. Being sensitive means that you read your and others' emotions better than most people do. This can be genetic and/or emotional genetics, such as when "Good" Kids are trained by their Bad Parent to attend to the emotions of others.

One of the things that I've experienced myself as well as seen in others is that being sensitive can cause social anxiety. This comes from being aware of all of the unspoken interpersonal emotional nuances going on around you in social settings, with no clear process for dealing with all of that information. The anger about being in such a situation can fuel anxiety.

Frequently anxiety is an indication of being out of touch

with feelings, and that you have a lot of unresolved anger to go along with old injuries. Most of my clients that suffer from anxiety are substantially locked into their "Good" Kids and, as a result, have no idea what they are feeling. One way for the "Bad" Kid to get the attention of their "Good" Kid is to shake up the system pretty severely. An anxiety attack or a panic attack can certainly shake your system, right to the foundation. Think back to George, the honeymooner whose story opened this book, and you can see how serious a panic attack can be.

Anger is a secondary emotion to the pain of an injury. Fear is another feeling that follows the pain. The feelings of anger and fear are a natural part of life. They are with us on a daily basis, though most of us tune them out unconsciously. For example, while driving, we don't focus on the fact that any driver coming from the opposite direction could easily kill us. We assume that they will not. We ignore that low level of anxiety (though this is not true for those who suffer from driving phobias and/or various other anxiety disorders). The fact that we have to deal with some level of anxiety in our lives on a regular basis is part of what makes anxiety so insidious.

Anxiety is different than depression, which, while incredibly common, is not a normal, healthy feeling. In some ways, the fact that fear is a normal part of life makes anxiety more difficult to deal with and more complex than depression. I often compare the relationship between depression and anxiety to the relationship between alcoholism and compulsive overeating. With alcoholism, you can stop drinking alcohol entirely. However, with compulsive overeating, you are faced with the fact that you still have to eat; the question is "How much?" Depression is not an emotion that you have to accept, while fears are a normal part of life. With anxiety disorders, we are faced with the question of "How much fear do I accept as reasonable and realistic?"

In working with the anxiety disorder called Post-Traumatic Stress Disorder (PTSD), I have noticed a process that develops which I call the PTSD Shunt. The PTSD Shunt is when anger is diverted into exaggerating fear, causing anxiety. It is central to PTSD in the sense that, in trauma, people are exposed to injuries that either do not allow them to safely use their anger to respond to it or are so overwhelming they feel as if their anger is ineffective and therefore worthless. This latter aspect can also be depressive in nature, in that people learn to be hopeless about their ability to use their anger for power.

If you imagine a young child who is being victimized or threatened by a parent, you can surely understand the idea that the child is being emotionally injured. This injury results in the simultaneous development of the three secondary emotions: sadness, fear, and anger. Fear is the most strongly present, followed by the anger and then the sadness. However, the child is in a situation where any expression of its anger is likely to result in further injury or even death. Sadness will be least likely to cause further injury to the child, then fear. The most likely emotion to elicit further damage is anger. The energy from the anger has to go somewhere, so it joins with the fear and exaggerates it.

Both the fear and the anger are related to fight or flight, and involved with adrenaline. This is quite different than sadness, which is quieter and less active. Thus the energy from the anger is "shunted," or transferred, into a more intense anxiety, or fear, experience. This exaggerated fear—anxiety—may cause physical, emotional, and cognitive "freezing," which are common experiences for someone suffering from PTSD. Samantha's case, which I'll describe next, will provide a window to see childhood trauma and its PTSD effects on the adult lives of survivors.

## Samantha's Story

Samantha grew up in a family where her father, Nathan, was bipolar and suffered from explosive anger. He would act out his anger during his more manic stages by yelling and screaming and breaking things. Her mother, Liz, was an alcoholic. Liz would get drunk and leave the family for days at a time. It wasn't clear whose problems initiated the conflicts, but they were loud, violent, and never really resolved. In addition, Liz would have affairs with men she met during her drinking binges. At times, she would return home with them, causing even greater conflicts between Nathan, herself, and the men she would bring home.

Nathan physically assaulted Liz a few times. On at least three separate occasions Liz responded by getting a handgun and threatening to shoot everyone. During one incident, she actually fired the gun. No one was hurt, but the police were called. No one was arrested since this was back before the days where there were laws about domestic violence, and everyone had quieted down by the time the police arrived. After these fights, Nathan would then settle into a quiet yet significant depression.

Samantha was the youngest of Nathan and Liz's three children. Her brother was an alcoholic, and her older sister had been married three times and was the single mother of two children by different fathers. Samantha had been in therapy at least six times over twenty years before she came into treatment with me. She had been hospitalized in her early twenties for alcohol abuse, having a blood alcohol level of 0.42—more than five times the usual legal limit for driving. Half of the people with a level of 0.50 are dead. Samantha had been incoherent and combative. After that hospitalization, she successfully avoided alcohol. She was on antidepressants and tranquilizers for a number of years, which helped her to be stable. She had been in and out of many relationships, but had withdrawn from relationships for two years prior to coming in to see me.

Samantha had ongoing anxiety problems and was vulnerable to bouts of depression. In spite of these problems, she had been able to make a good living as a real estate agent. When she came in to see me, at the age of forty-three, she was semi-retired, but owned a number of rental properties, which afforded her a comfortable income. However, she struggled in her relationships. She was always angry with or suspicious about someone, and periodically would suffer from panic attacks.

In her previous therapy, she was focused on addressing the immediate, symptomatic problems of anger, paranoia (a distrust of others in general), depression, and panic attacks. While these treatments helped her through rough times, her difficulties always seemed to return. She came to me with the agenda of healing. We worked extensively on her past, focusing on beginning to come to terms with the emotional injuries of growing up in a truly life-threatening environment. She had had a Category Two childhood.

At times we would deal with her anger toward her parents and at other times her fears. Frequently, as Samantha became more comfortable with the level of trust in our relationship, she would also touch on her sadness about not having been nurtured and pro-tected in her home. We would discuss the need for her to have her nervous system soothed by finding ways for her to be "off duty" emotionally, in her life and in her relationships.

There is significant data available now about the semi-per-manent impact of trauma on developing nervous systems. There is little doubt that there is physical impact on trauma survivors' ner-vous systems, which have been maintained in a state of hyper vig-ilance for an extensive period of time. Part of treatment requires the recuperation and resuscitation of a survivor's nervous system. This is why medication treatments can be so helpful for someone with a serious PTSD childhood.

I talked to Samantha about John Briere's concept of the ther-apeutic window, of finding the right amount of emotional stimu-lation in working with old trauma. I did this because to recover from PTSD, which Samantha needed to do, the body needs to process emotions that were put on hold in order to survive at the time of the trauma. However, the challenge is to revisit these emotions without having them become overwhelming. This can be challenging and requires the sensitivity of the therapist and the cooperation of the client. The process whereby the client and therapist work together to try to monitor the amount of emotional stimulation and the readi-ness of the client to attempt to reprocess difficult emotions is very important. It takes a good alliance between the therapist and client, and usually is only attempted after there is a good level of trust in place.

Sometimes attending to the therapeutic window doesn't work, no matter how thoughtful and sensitive the treatment alliance. At times, the client becomes overwhelmed emotionally. When this happens it requires a great deal of attention and care from the therapist. Medication can also play a central role in allowing the nervous system to settle down while these difficult there-and-then feelings are attended to in the here and now of treatment. In extreme situations, hospitalization can provide a safe environment for people who become too overwhelmed.

Samantha was able to re-experience her difficult feelings in the context of our caring and supportive therapy relationship. She had already established an ongoing medication regime, though as we worked on some of her more emotionally provocative memories, she needed some adjustment. Over time, she began to be able to relax more and more and actually decreased the amount of medication she used. Eventually, after three years in therapy, she was able to meet a man and begin what turned out to be a satisfying relationship. After the initial adjustment period in the relationship, her anger and anxiety settled down, and she and her partner did quite well.

While Samantha's example is one of severe PTSD, any threat to a child's nurturing can feel powerful, even if the threat is not intense in reality. If parents, giants who have the power of life and death over you, become threatening, you feel your life to be at risk. The child can experience the threat even if that isn't the intention of the parent. There are many examples of children who fail to thrive simply from not being loved. Beyond food and shelter and protection, to thrive we all need to have a sense of being loved and wanted.

Understanding your anxiety may require the help of a good therapist. You can see that your anxiety is likely to relate to the injuries, fears, and angers from your past in some way. Whether it relates to the family in which you grew up (as it usually does), your genetics and/or to later experiences, it's likely that you have some unresolved feelings. In order to complete the third part of the process, recovering from anxiety, you need to complete the second step, understanding what it is all about, and what it is that you really need to recover from.

## Step Three: Recovery

Recovery requires working through the emotions that underlie the problematic anxiety. You must give your body and your emotional being the chance in the here and now to process emotions that have been on hold since the original injury. This entails working through a process that is focused on allowing your body to deal with feelings that were put on hold, usually including the anger that has piggy-backed onto the fears. You may use role-playing techniques, Stop, Drop, and Roll, journaling, art therapy, or simply talk about it in therapy. It may very well involve working with the anger dysfunction in the internalized Bad Parent, "Good" Kid, and "Bad" Kid triangle. Ultimately, the unbending of the anger in recovering from anxiety focuses on taking the anger out of the extremely painful and self-abusive anxiety loop and turning it back into power.

Recovery can take many different forms, depending on the type of anxiety problem with which you are dealing. For example, a person suffering from Post-Traumatic Stress Disorder is likely to have a more complex and different recovery than that of someone suffering from a simple phobia. They both require confronting fears; however, a simple phobia responds much more quickly to therapy than an ingrained trauma.

This step, recovery, frequently requires psychotherapy, but that depends on the level of anxiety you are struggling with. Even if you only have mild anxiety, the recovery process is likely to be greatly facilitated by using a skilled therapist to help you through the process of identifying what is really going on. This healing process requires getting in touch with feelings and beginning to put them into the perspective of your emotional history. In the case of serious problems, like severe PTSD, it may require a full healing process, in which the dysfunctional anger process in the internal Bad Parent, "Good" Kid, and "Bad" Kid triangle is worked on until the hole in your heart is healed. The anger is used to change your internal, dysfunctional system until you have a solid Good Parent who communicates well with a "Good" Kid/"Bad" Kid team that works together (see Chapter Eight). In less serious levels of anxiety problems, a full emotional healing of childhood injuries may not be required. These kinds of problems can be resolved with some combination of medication, relaxation, and/or some form of psychotherapy.

## Bob's Story

An example of this would be Bob, a forty-three-year-old man, happily married for twenty-three of those years, and the father of two young adults. Bob is a low-level executive in a tech company. His father, Richard, was tyrannical and abusive. Richard's abuse of Bob was both physical and emotional, and he was narcissistic. While he wasn't a severe alcoholic, he drank regularly, and the abuse would worsen during those times. Bob's mother, Sylvia, was intimidated by Richard and suffered from her own feelings of inadequacy. She allowed her husband's behavior to go unchallenged.

Additionally, Sylvia directed her anger at her husband toward her son Bob because he was male and small enough so that she could exercise her power with him safely. Bob was the oldest of four children in that family and fell into the "Good" Kid caretaking role to survive the abuse of both his mother and father. Their abuse couldn't be avoided but the intensity decreased as he learned to jump to their every command.

Bob first came to me suffering from a severe level of depression along with bouts of intense anxiety, which found physical expression in the form of Irritable Bowel Syndrome (IBS). IBS is a common problem for those suffering from anxiety, which can cause sudden and intense experiences with severe diarrhea. He had become anorexic and hadn't eaten in four days. Bob was hospitalized briefly to get on medication and get his body accustomed to using food again. Once out of the hospital, he continued in therapy for a while, but gradually drifted out as his medications helped him to cope.

Three years later, his anxiety, IBS, and depression acted up again, and Bob returned to therapy. This was another brief round of treatment, as he increased his dosage of his antidepressant to get relief via medication.

Three years after his second round of treatment, he returned once again, still suffering from the same general problems, but not as severely as when he first came into treatment. At this time I asked Bob if he was committed to healing his problem, as opposed to working through a short-term treatment. He said that he was willing to confront the underlying problem.

As therapy unfolded, he worked on his unfinished anger with his father and mother, but seemed to be making little progress in dealing with his anxiety and IBS. In fact, as therapy progressed, these issues seemed to be getting progressively worse, and Bob was beginning to get more depressed.

Eventually, Bob admitted to me that he had had an affair in the early years of his marriage, when he'd been traveling quite a bit for work. At the time, his wife was preoccupied with their two young children and hadn't shown Bob much attention, sexual or otherwise. He was tearfully remorseful and overwhelmed with guilt. Because he was such a "Good" Kid, he had been tormenting himself with guilt over this secret mistake for more than twenty years.

I helped him to put it into perspective. He had acted out his anger in a manner that was destructive to himself and to his marriage. I helped him see that this anger was not meant to be directed against himself in the forms of anxiety, IBS, and depression. His real guilt (not neurotic) was being used in a neurotic and self-punishing manner that was extremely angry. Both the affair and the subsequent self-abuse were reflections of his anger with his father and mother. Having the affair was definitely a rebellious, "Bad" Kid thing to do. The reasons for it were related to his sense of being taken for granted by his wife during the first few years of his marriage, as well as his old angers with his father and mother.

Bob asked if he should tell his wife about the affair from twenty years earlier. I said that it was his choice; however, that I thought telling his wife would be an angry and selfish thing to do. He would be telling her so that she would forgive him, not to take care of her in any way. Bob would be injuring her further to salve his own conscience.

Once the secret was disclosed to me, Bob was able to begin to stop punishing himself with anxiety. Gradually, the anxiety and IBS went further and further into remission, and he was able to stop treatment without a full healing process.

Recovery requires some level of dealing with the feelings related to the injury or injuries that have yet to be processed. In Bob's case, this processing meant spending time dealing with the painful guilt that was really a distorted version of his anger toward his father and mother. In understanding the way in which his anger for his parents influenced his acting out his anger inappropriately in his marriage, he was able to begin to come to terms with his mistake and forgive himself. He didn't remain stuck with the self-definition with which he had been living, that of a liar and a cheat.

Self-definitions can be *very* limiting for people in their growth processes. I like to tell my clients about the time I shoplifted a can of shoe polish from Woolworth's when I was eight. An employee caught me outside and proceeded to scare me half to death by threatening to tell my parents. (I hope they don't read this.) It cured me of continuing to shoplift. Even though I had shoplifted, this experience doesn't sentence me to having to keep the definition of being a thief for the rest of my life. I like to think of psychotherapy as a chance to redefine oneself and to examine the definitions you've had in the past as a part of that process of change.

In Bob's case, he came to realize that his affair from twenty-plus years ago did not have to define him as a liar and a cheat. He still regretted the dysfunctional uses of his anger but was able to finally forgive himself and let go of those definitions as he understood what they were about.

In Samantha's case, recovery involved spending a great deal of time in working with the anger, fears, and pain related to severe abuse and chaos in her childhood home. We often returned to her feelings of being abandoned in childhood, which seemed to have little immediate connection with her current life. We used role-playing techniques (Gestalt therapy) as well as Eye Movement Desensitization and Reprocessing techniques (EMDR). We spent time with the actual painful feelings in her past as well as envisioned and imagined what her past could have and should have been like. As she spent time with both the painful memories and the positive fantasies, she was able to put them into a better perspective. She also was able to stop blaming herself. She began to direct the anger she felt toward her parents into her healing process, and even was able to pursue a healthy relationship.

I have tremendous respect for the courage that my clients display in tackling old and difficult emotions. In my experience, as well as that of my clients, the process frequently is driven by a sense of desperation. Anxiety can and will make your life miserable if you let it. It will exaggerate your fears and steal the bulk of your life. The importance and difficulty of facing your fears cannot be overstressed. This idea is captured in another quote I like, this one from Bertrand Russell, who was awarded the Nobel Prize in 1950. He said "those who fear life are already three parts dead." Living a life that is mostly dead is not acceptable. The very energy of the distorted anger that has fueled the self-abusive anxiety can, and must, empower you to gain the recovery that you deserve.

# CHAPTER 5

# Anger and Mood Disorders

## Depression Is a Parasite

DEPRESSION IS A PARASITE THAT CAPTURES THE LIGHT in your life, darkens your soul, and sucks out all your joy. It can come on slowly, the way a parasite steals nutrients from your body, gradually weakening it over time. It can appear forcefully and quickly if you experience some major life injury and don't have the support you need to deal with it.

Most people who come in for treatment for a mood disorder usually have had a number of significant and recent life injuries. Additionally, most of us have some early childhood injuries that play a role in experiencing a major depression. It is not unusual to have also some degree of an underlying diagnosis of Post-Traumatic Stress Disorder, since early childhood injuries often feel life threatening even if they are not. Childhood injuries can have a serious impact on an innocent child.

Anger plays a central role in major depression and in all depressive behavior. Therapists define depression as anger turned against the self, combined with a sense of hopelessness or helplessness. You can see this in some of the classic depressive thoughts like "I don't deserve anything good in my life" or "I'm worthless." If you look closely, you can see the self-directed anger contained in these thoughts. When depressive thoughts are said out loud, as if they were said to someone else, you can see how angry they sound. The thoughts become "You don't deserve anything good in your life!" and "You're worthless!" Those are mean and angry things to say to someone.

Remember the concept of *unbending anger* from Chapter Two—anger must be directed in a positive manner, away from your self, regardless of what healthy use you put it to. In order to recover from depression, you must learn to use your anger for what it was meant: self-nurturing or power. Self-nurturing means using your anger to do something that directly takes care of you. Power means using your anger to act on the world in a way that causes it to take care of you. Putting your anger to use definitely does not mean that you should take out your anger on some one else or hurt someone. Most of the time, those other-destructive behaviors are also self-destructive. They lower your self-esteem.

Tom, one of my clients, clearly manifested this dynamic. Tom had tremendous anger for his father, who had beaten him throughout his childhood. Tom had no idea how angry he was, but he would go to bars, drink a lot, and then pick fights with strangers. When I met Tom, he had been put in jail for a fight in which he had blinded a young man in one eye. Tom had acted out his anger on this unsuspecting victim by hitting him in the face with a beer bottle. Afterwards, Tom became depressed and suicidal because he felt so guilty. Frequently, when we act out our anger on others, it cycles back against us in the form of real guilt.

Like all emotions, anger has both energy and information. Anger, like sadness and fear, are secondary emotions. There is always an injury and pain that comes first, and the anger is meant to fix what is hurting you. In depression, the anger is not working to fix what is hurting you. It has become fixed into a loop where it works against you and then you come to believe that your condition is hopeless.

In this chapter I will give you tools to help you determine if you have a major depression or a bipolar disorder. Please consult with a mental health professional if you believe you have either problem or simply to help clarify your diagnosis. I'll also help you to understand the roles that anger can play in both the dysfunction and moving toward healing.

## Indicators of Major Depression

When I use the word *depression*, I'm talking about a depressive disorder. Depression as a mood disorder is different and usually more serious than when people say in normal conversation that they're depressed. When a therapist diagnoses major depression, it means that for at least two weeks an individual has had at least five of nine criteria, or specific behaviors, that are signs of depression.

As you read the criteria below, keep in mind that if you think you have depression, you need to consult with a qualified mental health professional to verify your diagnosis.

Probably the most obvious indication of someone who's struggling with major depression is that more than half of the feelings or emotions that they experience are negative—feelings such as sadness, anger, pain, or jealousy.

Another indication is having trouble sleeping. This might mean that you sleep all the time and never seem to be rested or it could mean that you're not getting enough sleep or having a hard time getting to sleep and/or staying asleep. Any of these would give you one of the nine criteria that would lead to a diagnosis of depression.

The next criterion would be that during the same two-week period you also experienced a loss of interest or pleasure in things that you previously enjoyed, things like hobbies or other fun activities. You also lack the motivation to pursue those interests.

Another important criterion is if you find yourself feeling worthless or guilty without real cause or you experience low self-esteem. Again, you would need to have any of these indicators going on for a minimum of two weeks.

When people are seriously depressed, they also find that they struggle with finding the energy they need to complete their normal daily tasks. If your work or personal life suffers, when you find that you just don't have the get up and go to actually get up and *do*, it means you could have some diagnosable depression.

Another criterion, one that's related to the previous indicator, is that of concentration. When you find that you just can't concentrate on the tasks you need to accomplish, it could mean that you're in trouble. Whether it's reading or some other focused task, you might find that you're not able to keep your thoughts from straying. This can be a function of either distraction, when you find your thoughts drifting off from the task at hand to other random thoughts or activities, or what's called rumination, a thinking process in which you keep going over and over something. Usually the focus is something painful or upsetting. Either of these problems can lead to difficulty concentrating, which would mean you would endorse this criterion.

Another indication of depression is when you have problems with your appetite. Similarly to when we talked about sleep problems, you can have either too little or too much of an appetite. This same concept about appetite applies to sexual appetite as well. If the desire for sexual contact either increases or decreases significantly, that can be a sign of problems with depression.

The next group of indicators relates to one's normal state of stimulation or arousal. If you find yourself being agitated or jittery and having a hard time sitting or standing still, this may be another sign of depression. Just as when we were looking at appetite and sleep, the reverse can be an indicator as well. That means that if you find yourself being lethargic and having difficulty getting going, it could be a reason to be concerned as well.

The last criterion to consider is suicidal thinking. To consider if this is a problem, you would need to examine your thought process. A major concern is if you have a plan for suicide or clearly suicidal thoughts. However, morbidity—when you find yourself thinking a lot about death or even just drawn to notice and focus on decay in your surroundings—would be an indication of a positive criterion for depression as well.

To sum up, consider the nine areas described above to see if you have five that you feel have been going on for at least two weeks. If you have five of the criteria, then you have a mild level of major depression; seven would be a moderate level of major depression; and nine indicate severe depression. If you have even a mild level of major depression, you would be wise to seek help. I would also recommend that you begin to use the Stop, Drop, and Roll technique (from Chapter Two) right away to begin to use your anger functionally and beat back the depression.

## Simon's Story

To understand how to work the Stop, Drop, and Roll steps with major depression, let's look at Simon Jones. Simon was sinking fast. He could barely sleep and was irritable all the time. He could hardly concentrate on work and most days he didn't even want to get out of bed. He didn't know it yet, but he was in the midst of a major depression.

What had happened to his life? He must have asked himself that question a thousand times in the last week alone. Only six months ago he was living with his wife, Sondra, and their three children. All of the kids were finally in school, and Sondra had more time and felt like she had a life of her own. Simon had a good reputation in the black community, and they were living the American Dream. Simon was finally beginning to be successful after twenty years of selling insurance in Philadelphia. He was really nice to people, and that was the key to his gradual success in sales. Everyone liked him.

Yet here he was, only six months after their family vacation in Disneyland, sitting in a strange furnished apartment, feeling lost and lonely. He didn't want to be divorced. He didn't want to be separated from his kids. He was lost.

Sondra had kicked him out only two months after they'd returned home from Disneyland. They'd had a fight about nothing in particular, and she'd just gone off the deep end. Simon had kind of gotten used to Sondra's moods. She was demanding and nothing he did ever seemed to be good enough for her. She'd always been pretty particular about how she wanted things to be around their home and in their life, but ever since they had kids, she seemed to find Simon to be unacceptable. She disapproved of the way he related to the kids and behaved around the house. He'd begun to think that he couldn't even breathe right.

Their latest fight was about sex. He didn't seem to ever really please her in that area, either. It seemed like most of the time Sondra just wasn't interested, and when she was, she always ended up disappointed. Simon was so afraid of her disapproval that he'd just about stopped initiating sexual contact or asking for anything else.

But Simon enjoyed spending time with his kids, taking them to their sports activities, giving the younger ones baths, and reading to them in the evenings. He even cooked dinner much of the time, since Sondra seemed to be so overwhelmed at the end of the day. These changes meant that Simon had retreated from Sondra more and more over the years as the kids had grown. He watched sports and read his murder mysteries and developed his clientele.

He'd known that he and Sondra really weren't close, but when she demanded that he leave, he was totally surprised.

When Sondra kicked him out, Simon's male friends were shocked. Sondra's female friends weren't surprised at all since Sondra had been complaining about Simon to them for years. They were mostly stay-at-home moms like Sondra. Simon and Sondra's friends who had marriages where the wife worked disapproved of Sondra. Since Simon had been so successful, Sondra really didn't need to work. However, she seemed to always complain about him, even when they socialized, which made for some awkward moments at parties.

Simon and Sondra came from vastly different backgrounds. Simon was an only child. His father, Marcus, had died of cancer when Simon was eleven. Luckily, Simon's mother, Elizabeth, had a college degree and a good job as a legal assistant, so she was able to support the family. Though his mom worked and he had to be the man of the family early on, he rose to the task and didn't get involved in gangs or some of the other trouble that some of his friends drifted into.

In contrast, Sondra's family was a mess. She grew up poor and was exposed to physical and emotional abuse from her father, Jack, and her uncle, Roger, who were both alcoholics and drug users. She was also sexually abused by her uncle Roger. Sondra's mother, Elaine, worked as a servant in one of the wealthy white homes in the suburbs and was gone all day, every day. While Elaine knew that Jack and Roger had problems, she didn't know what to do about the physical and emotional abuse. Elaine didn't even know about the sexual abuse until it was too late. She tried to protect her children by having her younger sister, Gloria, come and stay in their home to look after the five kids.

Unfortunately, Gloria was young and impressionable, and Jack and Roger enticed her into using drugs and alcohol. Elaine didn't realize that this was happening. Soon Gloria was having sex with both Jack and Roger when Elaine was at work, an arrangement that went on for a number of years. Elaine had no idea about that, either.

During that time, Sondra, who was eleven and the oldest of the children, was exposed to Roger's sexual advances. Sondra hadn't gotten much attention as a young girl. The sexual contact felt good in and of itself, and she enjoyed the attention. She did have a vague feeling that what she was doing wasn't right, but she had no one to turn to.

Once Elaine found out about what had been going on under her nose, she threw out the adults, but the damage had been done to the children. Sondra grew up confused, angry, and afraid. She wondered if it was her fault that her father was kicked out. She also felt embarrassed when she began to get noticed by the boys at school. She ended up being promiscuous early in her teens. After a while, however, she realized that she didn't need to be sexual in order to have boys interested in her.

Sondra had thought that she had put all of that childhood stuff behind her, but when she and Simon started having children, she found herself being tired, uninterested in sex, and resentful of Simon's advances. She felt unappreciated and overwhelmed. She began to resent Simon's being away from home all the time. While those kind of feelings are not unusual for mothers with young children, Sondra's were stronger than most, since they resonated with her feelings of being left at home by her mother.

Simon and Sondra weren't aware that she was suffering from both Post-Traumatic Stress Disorder and major depression. Simon just assumed that she was irritable from sleep deprivation and thought it was normal that she was less interested in sex after having babies. It was normal for him to be a caretaker of a woman—he'd been trained to do that with his mother. Until Sondra had asked him to leave, he never suspected that she saw his presence as unnecessary and unwanted.

Sondra didn't think anything was wrong with her. She knew that all of the problems were really Simon's—he just didn't do enough or understand how stressed she was. She was confused by her feelings when they had sex and wanted to ignore all of the emotions that got stirred up. Sondra ended up hating Simon, not understanding that most of her feelings about him were related to her childhood and the adults who had abandoned and abused her. Although she wasn't aware of it, she was terrified of those feelings. She wouldn't even consider counseling.

Simon didn't think of counseling either. But his mother recognized his depression after four months of the separation. He showed many of the classic signs of depression. He seemed down. He was withdrawn and didn't look good. He was losing weight and always seemed tired. He put on a pretty good front, but his mother could tell that something was wrong. She sent him to the social worker that she had seen after his father had died. Mrs. Abernathy had a great deal of experience and a kind and gentle soul. Although reluctant, Simon agreed to see her.

## Stop, Drop, and Roll

In their first meeting, Mrs. Abernathy was able to identify that Simon had enough criteria to fulfill a diagnosis for major depression. She also knew about the Stop, Drop, and Roll technique, and she discussed the steps with Simon, explaining that depression was anger turned against oneself. She encouraged him to begin to work on identifying his anger.

Simon left the first session feeling relieved, but also a little overwhelmed and confused. He was relieved because he realized that Mrs. Abernathy could help him, but she offered so much information in such a short period of time that he couldn't really begin to take it all in.

In their next meeting, Mrs. Abernathy spoke some more about anger and depression and how he could dig himself out. Together they decided the first step, Stop, was to identify his depressive thoughts and feelings and then take a time out. Mrs. Abernathy helped Simon to see that he was angry with Sondra for dumping him and having been so distant from him for so long. Mrs. Abernathy assigned him the task of beginning a journal so he could track both his feelings and progress as he began to work his way out of his depression.

Simon quickly realized that identifying his feelings was a problem for him, though he didn't know why. He talked about this difficulty with Mrs. Abernathy in their next meeting. They realized that since the death of his father, Simon had been trained to take care of his mother, who was devastated. She didn't realize that she was asking Simon to protect her from his loss of a father. Simon got the message that he was supposed to take care of his mother's emotional needs and not attend to his own feelings. Simon was a typical "Good" Kid. Since he was unable to know what he was feeling, he couldn't complete the first step.

Simon had to work many weeks on recognizing his own emotions. He had to keep asking himself the question "What am I feeling right now?" over and over again. Eventually, with practice and writing in his journal, he began to come up with answers. He began to notice the sinking, depressive feelings, along with some self-abusive thoughts. He began to notice thinking things like "I deserve to be alone," "I'll never find anyone to love me," and "My kids are going to hate me." He found many other similar negative thoughts.

It took a few more weeks before Simon actually had his first success at not only noticing the feelings and thoughts, but also taking a time out. He found the second step, Drop, a lot more comfortable. Simon had been living in his head for most of his life, so the cognitive process of sorting through the questions about what he was angry about, and what was hurting him, was much easier than the first step of noticing his problematic feelings.

Mrs. Abernathy was very helpful in finding the answers to Simon's questions about his old injuries. He began to realize that the old injuries were all about his father's death. The loss of his father led him to feel abandoned, even though he knew his father hadn't intended to leave him at such young age. He began to see how he was psychologically attracted to Sondra because she was both distant and emotionally needy. This was a form of transference. Those aspects of Sondra resonated with Simon's loss of his father and his mother's distance because of her need to focus on work, as well as his training to take care of his mother emotionally.

Once Simon got over his initial shock and resistance, he thought that learning to think in these psychological ways was exciting. He struggled at first, because he didn't want to own these difficult feelings. How could he be angry with his father for dying? It didn't seem to be fair or make any rational sense. How could he be angry with his mother for being so distraught that her husband had died? He didn't want to accept these feelings, but he gradually began to see how they had caused him to struggle. Mrs. Abernathy also explained that he could be mad at his parents and still love them, validating these mixed feelings.

The third step, Roll, was slow to develop as well. Since Simon had spent so much of his time in the role of being the "Good" Kid, the idea of using his anger to increase his power felt threatening. It wasn't easy to realize what he needed to do with his anger and to feel comfortable taking those actions. Here, again, Mrs. Abernathy was quite helpful in aiding and encouraging Simon to identify what he needed to do and giving him permission to take action.

Simon needed to begin to deal with the reality of his separation and looming divorce. Sondra had already contacted an attorney and was asking for custody of the children, possession of the home, and significant maintenance. Basically, she wanted to have her life be exactly the same as before, with the subtraction of Simon.

When Mrs. Abernathy helped Simon realize his need to get an attorney and defend himself, he struggled. Even though he missed his kids terribly, he still felt that it was wrong to insist on a regular visitation schedule. Sondra acted as if it was an imposition to her if he wanted to see the kids and she seemed to be suspicious of Simon and his motives. She would call him to take care of the kids when it was convenient for her and wouldn't let them stay at his house overnight.

As Simon began to look at these dynamics with Mrs. Abernathy, he began to realize that not only was it not in his best interests to let this go on, but that it wasn't healthy for his children, either. When Simon consulted with an attorney, she only verified what he was feeling. After Simon brought up his concerns to Sondra, she became quite upset and threatened to never let him see the children again.

After this conflict, Simon talked with both Mrs. Abernathy and his attorney. They reassured him that Sondra couldn't prevent him from seeing the children and convinced him to let his lawyer communicate with Sondra until she calmed down.

In addition to Simon's taking charge of his visitation rights, another example of his Roll actions related to his housing. Mrs. Abernathy recommended that Simon rent an apartment that would be big enough for him and the kids. While Simon again hesitated, thinking that he would hurt the family's finances, he realized that the family's finances couldn't help but be impacted by the divorce, but that he nevertheless needed to be able to provide his version of home for his children.

Gradually, as Simon became more and more assertive, he found that he began to feel less depressed. It felt good to take care of himself. Plus, he realized that he had been repressing a large amount of anger for Sondra for a long time, and it felt good to stop denying those feelings, even if they weren't pleasant.

Eventually, over a period of several months, Simon was able to use Mrs. Abernathy's help and he got to the point where he wasn't depressed. He could use the Stop, Drop, and Roll system on his own. The divorce was under way, and he had begun to build his own support system. Simon could see the possibilities of life after divorce and even began to consider dating. He could conceive of having a relationship that would be much healthier than what he'd had with Sondra, even if he wasn't quite ready yet.

## The Role of Medication

In some ways, Simon was lucky. He'd had a major depression of mild to moderate levels and didn't need medication to fight his way out of it. In my experience, this is frequently, but not always, true for depressions of this magnitude. In situations where the magnitude is significantly greater, medication is usually recommended, if not necessary, for recovery.

Many people have a great resistance to taking medication. Frequently, it makes them feel as if they are truly "sick." There is, unfortunately, a stigma that makes it difficult for people to seek any kind of mental health help. That's why some people would rather take medication than have to talk to someone. They don't want to feel exposed by talking about the problems in their lives. But, on the other hand, most people don't like to have to take any medication. Many people experience the idea of medication as a further injury.

Unless someone is severely depressed, I usually don't insist on medication for my clients. I will generally discuss the idea with any sign of major depression. My recommendations become stronger and more frequent the more severe the level of depression and suffering.

Medications are tools, just like psychotherapy or this book, and I encourage my clients to think of them as such. Some people with even a severe major depression will recover over a period of years without medication, though this is unusual. Most will not recover spontaneously. Additionally, the longer you remain depressed, the more likely you are to become both more depressed and depressed again. This relates to both brain chemistry and to the impact of major depression on a person's life. When people are depressed, over time, things tend to get worse in their lives. Bad things tend to happen to them. They lose their jobs or their marriages. The increasing difficulty and injury of their lives then adds to the likelihood of becoming more depressed, so it can become a downward spiral. It's important not to allow that to continue. Besides using the appropriate medication, the Stop, Drop, and Roll system is a good place to start working to unbend the anger from depression into empowerment.

## Bipolar Disorder: It *Is* Possible To Feel Too Good

It's a misconception that the opposite of depression is a mania that feels good. Although sometimes people in a manic state really do feel too good, more often someone suffering from bipolar disorder is irritable, self-destructive, and very unstable. You can see the role that anger plays in self-destructive behavior, and irritability implies being very vulnerable to injury and to having angry outbursts. People suffering from mania also can be very irresponsible, which is a form of passive-aggressive anger because it draws the anger of others toward them. My experience is that frequently someone with a severe bipolar disorder is suffering as intensely as someone struggling with the extremes of anxiety.

Bipolar mood disorders include some level of major depression combined with significant mood swings. These mood swings may be intense enough to be diagnosed as either *hypo mania* or *mania*. Hypo mania is a mood state that is significantly elevated from normal, but does not qualify as full-blown mania. The difference is the degree of the mood swings; they are more intense in mania.

## Douglas' Story

Douglas was a good example of someone who was hypo manic. He owned a small trucking company and was married and had a two-year-old daughter. His wife, Helen, had worked in his business with him, but she'd decided to stay home with their daughter. Douglas had a history that included both depression and one episode of full-blown mania. When he came in for treatment, he had been off of medication for three and a half years and felt he was doing well. Helen disagreed, however, and wanted Douglas to come in for treatment.

Douglas was in a funk. His life was not terrible, but not really OK either. He was irritable and had a lot of conflict with Helen. He wasn't sleeping well, but he chalked that up to having a baby in the house. He loved his daughter and felt that she was the best thing in his life. However, his moods seemed to be brittle and could shift very quickly.

He was starting to feel that he had no friends. People in his business got along with him, but he felt he never really connected to others. He felt that, for the most part, that was their problem—he didn't see himself as having any problems. He also used marijuana on a regular basis. He didn't feel he was addicted to it, but felt he often had a poor mood without using it. He had also made a couple of recent business deals that didn't work out very well and looking back on them, he considered them to be foolish.

Over the course of treatment, it became clear that Douglas was depressed and having some hypo mania. His marijuana use seemed very clearly to be an attempt to self-medicate. I referred him to his old psychiatrist, who put him back on an antidepressant as well as a mood stabilizer. He improved fairly quickly after this medication intervention in spite of the fact that he thought nothing was wrong.

Douglas decided that he would maintain his medication regime when he discontinued psychotherapy. Anyone who is bipolar, at any level, would be well served to maintain medication throughout their lives. While having to take medication can be an injury, recent research suggests that late-stage bipolar disorder can be much harder to treat if the medication regime is not maintained.

## Signs of Mania

As I said earlier, many people think that mania is the opposite of depression, and sometimes it can be. People in a state of mania can experience an elevated or expansive mood; however, they also can experience an irritable mood or angry explosions. When a person intensely experiences any of these moods over a period of at least four days, they may qualify for a diagnosis of mania. But in order to do so, they must also have at least three of the following criteria, or four criteria if they are irritable and not elevated in their mood.

The first of these is a decreased need for sleep. People who are manic can get only three to five hours of sleep at night (or even less) and wake up feeling fully rested and refreshed, as opposed to feeling groggy, sleepy, and out of sorts. At times, since someone who is bipolar also experiences some level of major depression, they may struggle with sleep and find that it adds to their irritability.

Another sign of mania is significantly fast and/or pressured speech. People with mania may talk very rapidly or be unable to contain their need to communicate. It can be hard to get a word in edgewise when you're talking with them.

When someone is in a manic state, they may also experience one of the following: either the subjective experience that their mind is racing or what is called a "flight of ideas." A flight of ideas is when someone finds that he or she experiences a series of thoughts, each one leading to the next, that are usually very philosophical and far reaching. People in a manic state will frequently find that they may be thinking about the nature of the universe, God, the meaning of life—they even may believe that they are discovering all of the answers to mankind's incredibly complex questions. The experience will be similar to, but subjectively different from, an undergraduate who has taken a good religion or philosophy course and found it to be highly stimulating.

Another of the criteria for mania is distractibility. You may notice that someone suffering from mania may have his or her attention wander fairly erratically. Someone in full-blown mania will have trouble staying on task in a conversation. They may begin to discuss their family and end up noticing a picture on the wall, which may lead them to discuss art or other ideas. Talking to this individual can be quite dramatic and even frustrating.

One of the more frequently seen characteristics of someone in a manic state is goal-directed behavior. You might find someone in a manic state cleaning the kitchen floor at two o'clock in the morning with a toothbrush and having a great time. This kind of goal-directed energy could also be focused on work. It may be socially expressed, as he or she may be intensely planning a party or developing a certain friendship. It can even be expressed in compulsive sexual behavior.

Another criterion is grandiosity. This is an example of how mania can, indeed, be the opposite of major depression, which includes a feeling of worthlessness. In mania, it isn't unusual for the level of self-esteem to reverse. Someone can go from feeling totally worthless to feeling that they can do no wrong. One of the old caricatures of in-patients in mental hospitals was that they would think that they were Napoleon or Jesus Christ. In mania, if there is a psychotic aspect, these kinds of examples of extreme grandiosity can occur. Without that kind of psychotic component, people can just be extremely overconfident, which is much more common.

Finally, one of the most important criteria is that the individual can participate in extremely risky behavior without realizing the risk involved. They engage in behaviors that they would be extremely unlikely to do when not in a manic state. An example of this would be where a happily married man or woman goes out and initiates sexual affairs. Or, someone who isn't married may engage in frequent and unsafe sex. Another example would be where someone goes out and spends significant sums of money that they don't have. A person in a manic state might take physical risks, such as going rock climbing without any preparation or equipment.

If you have a period of time, at least four days, when you have three or more of these criteria, you should seek help. If your mood is irritable and not the elevated or high type, you would need four of these criteria to fit a diagnosis of mania or hypo mania. It would depend on the degree of intensity of the symptoms. If you are in any doubt, I would recommend a consultation with a mental health professional.

## Medication and Bipolar Mood Disorder

Medication frequently plays a major role in the treatment of a bipolar mood disorder. Unless someone has a very mild bipolar disorder, it would be very unusual not to need some form of medication to stabilize one's moods. When someone is suffering enough that they actually seek treatment, they usually are already in a significantly destabilized state.

A great thing is that many people who are truly suffering have a greater likelihood of finding relief from one of the many new medications available. Psychiatrists, as well as primary care physicians, prescribe medication more frequently. People who have mood swings that are problematic, but not severe enough to be considered disordered, may still benefit from the main class of medications used in treating bipolar disorder. These are called *mood stabilizers*.

Psychotropic medications are drugs that are prescribed to affect mood and anxiety. Antidepressants, mood stabilizers, tranquilizers, and antipsychotic medications are in this class of chemical compounds that can be prescribed. In recent years, family physicians have tended to prescribe more antidepressant medications. One of the downsides of this practice is that antidepressants, which are very helpful in treating depression and anxiety, can trigger mania when it is latent or hidden. This means that sometimes when someone is depressed and takes an antidepressant medication, but they also have an undiagnosed bipolar disorder, the antidepressant can push them into mania. This can be very upsetting to someone who hasn't been aware of the underlying bipolar problem, and to his or her family. This kind of triggering of a latent mania occurs infrequently, but it can, and does, happen.

What makes all this even more confusing is that someone who is bipolar may find that a mood stabilizer helps them, but that they may still need the additional help provided by an antidepressant. This is done when someone has their mood stabilized, but they are stabilized in a depressed state. If someone is in the later stages of bipolar disorder, they may find that they have three or four medications prescribed, including an antipsychotic. Antipsychotics are not only prescribed for psychosis, which means being out of touch with reality. They are also called *major tranquilizers* and may be prescribed, along with a mood stabilizer and an antidepressant, to help the client settle down.

The complications which can be involved in treating bipolar disorder with medication are why, in general, I recommend involving a psychiatrist. Psychiatrists specialize in treating mental health problems with medication, so they tend to be more knowledgeable than primary care physicians, even though many primary care doctors are quite knowledgeable as well.

## Sheila's Story

The case of Sheila McCarthy provides an opportunity for us to examine the roles of anger and psychotherapy in treating bipolar disorder.

Sheila was coming apart. At thirty-two, she hated what she'd become. She acted like a shrew with her husband, Ray, and wasn't much better with their two young children, Sarah, four, and Terry, eighteen months old.

Sheila was bright, a hard worker, and very much a "people person." She had been a successful stockbroker at a prestigious firm on Wall Street. That was where she had met Ray, then a junior analyst. They had both been on the fast track when they met, fell in love, and married.

Sheila and Ray had discussed having children and agreed that it would be best for Sheila to take a few years off so that the kids could have a full-time mom. They had prepared financially, and Ray was doing very well both at work and with their own investments.

Sheila had suffered from a mild postpartum depression after Sarah's birth, but it had lasted only a few months. She recovered on her own after talking about it with her doctor and some friends. She worked out some ways to get a little time to herself and eventually felt a lot better.

When Terry was born a few years later, she was fine at first. She'd had a Caesarian section and stayed in the hospital for ten days to recover from the surgery. After a few weeks at home, however, she began to wear down and move into a sleep-deprived, irritable state. Gradually, as the reality of life at home with two little kids sank in, she found that she was becoming more and more depressed. After about six months of misery, Ray insisted that she talk to their family doctor.

Dr. David Meyers was in family medicine, and, after talking with Sheila, put her on one of the newer antidepressant medications. When Sheila began taking it, it didn't seem to do much, but gradually, after about six weeks, she noticed she was feeling a little better. After talking again with Dr. Meyers, they decided to increase her dose. After another month she began to feel much better. She had lots of energy, and it didn't seem to be such a burden to take care of the kids.

However, there was a brittle aspect to her moods. If something didn't go her way, her good mood could evaporate in an instant, and she would either become very quiet or lash out. Sheila was still pretty irritable with Ray and the kids, and when she would get angry, she would really lose it, yelling and screaming. It was like a wave of emotion that just had to run its course until she calmed down. When she was calm, she felt terribly sorry and guilty. Gradually, it seemed as though her self-esteem had only two positions, on or off.

Sheila began to think that her medication wasn't working well enough and that she needed to take more. She decided to take an extra pill every time she went though one of her down, remorseful periods.

Sheila and Ray were pretty sociable and before they'd had children, they had hung around with a crowd who were pretty heavy drinkers. Once she was pregnant, Sheila stopped drinking entirely. Ray, being a supportive husband, stopped drinking as well. After the pregnancies, they had started drinking again socially. As Sheila's moods started improving with her medication, she started drinking more heavily with their friends. A couple of times she got really trashed. After this would happen, she would go through a guilt cycle just like the ones she would have after she'd blown up.

After a while, Sheila started drinking at home by herself after some of her angry outbursts. She wouldn't get really drunk. She thought it improved her mood. Gradually, however, her mood swings began to get sharper and sharper. A few times, Ray came home to find her slurring her words and when he confronted her, it would set off another angry explosion.

Things came to a head when Sheila stormed out of the house after one of these angry confrontations. When she didn't come home that night, Ray was frantic.

When she called Ray the next morning, he came and got her. They found the family minivan parked near the bar that she'd gone to in her rage. Sheila didn't remember anything until she had awakened in a motel the next morning with a strange man next to her in bed.

Ray and Sheila were both devastated. Initially, at least, Ray wasn't sure that he even wanted to stay in the marriage. He thought she was becoming an alcoholic. Sheila didn't know what to think but she certainly felt horribly guilty. She felt as if she didn't even know herself anymore. She immediately stopped drinking and swore that she would never allow anything like that to happen again. She was terrified, especially about the possibility of losing Ray and the kids, and didn't trust herself.

Unfortunately, Sheila's mood swings seemed to be getting worse and worse. She would live her life in a seemingly comfortable state, and Ray would think that things were better. However, underneath the surface, Sheila was hiding her depressions from Ray. She would pretend that everything was fine while, in reality, she was in despair. This would last for maybe four or five days until she couldn't stand it anymore, and then she would blow up in a big way over something minor. At times she would be laughing hysterically one minute and then sobbing the next. She seemed to be sleeping less and less on some days, and then, on other days, couldn't even get out of bed.

Sheila and Ray were pretty private people, not used to sharing a lot about their personal lives, but Ray knew that he was in over his head. It was time to go back to Dr. Meyers.

Dr. Meyers was surprised to see them doing so poorly. He had been prescribing the antidepressant and had assumed that everything was going well. He hadn't heard any complaints, even when he had asked during their well-baby checkups. Once he heard some of their problems, he realized that it was necessary for Sheila to consult with a psychiatrist.

Ray and Sheila met with Dr. Steinberg, the psychiatrist who was recommended by Dr. Meyers. Dr. Steinberg spent about an hour and a half with them and asked lots of questions so that she could understand exactly what Sheila had been doing and experiencing. She also asked about Sheila's family history and found that, indeed, both Sheila's mother and her grandmother had experienced some level of depression. Her grandmother had even been in a mental hospital at one point. Dr. Steinberg diagnosed Sheila as having a mild to moderate bipolar disorder. Dr. Steinberg had Sheila gradually begin to reduce the amount of antidepressant medication she'd been taking. She asked Sheila to be sure to follow her directions about how to take her medication. Dr. Steinberg also told

Sheila to completely avoid alcohol, since alcohol can destabilize someone who is taking medications for mood by washing it out of the body. She also had Sheila start taking a mood stabilizing medication. Since mood stabilizers work more quickly than antidepressants, Sheila began to notice some relief after her first week on the new medication.

Sheila met with Dr. Steinberg about ten days later for about forty-five minutes. Dr. Steinberg was pleased that Sheila was beginning to respond to the mood stabilizer. Dr. Steinberg's plan was to follow closely Sheila's progress with medication for at least the first two months, but she felt that Sheila was in need of some individual and conjoint counseling. Dr. Steinberg referred Sheila to a psychologist, Dr. Weinstrand.

Sheila saw Dr. Weinstrand alone for the first meeting. In that meeting, Dr. Weinstrand got to know Sheila a little bit and began to understand her problems. He also got her history and the history of her family of origin. At their second meeting, he began to discuss anger, depression, and bipolar disorder with Sheila.

Sheila's mother, Joyce, had been depressed when she was growing up, somewhat related to Sheila's grandmother. Joyce's own mother was bipolar and had been hospitalized when Sheila was quite young. Dr. Weinstrand talked about how Joyce's depression may have made her unavailable both physically and emotionally to Sheila. He discussed how these kinds of injuries, which may be experienced somewhat subtly, can nonetheless result in anger. He also talked about how unexpressed or unused anger can turn inwards into depression. Even though bipolar depression has a physiological basis, it can be made worse by anger that isn't dealt with effectively.

In addition to the insights she gained from the talk therapy, Sheila was already beginning to feel significant improvement from the effects of her medication. She was reassured simply by realizing that she suffered from a real disorder that was treatable. Even though she didn't like the idea of having to take medications, she began to realize that these problems were not a function of her being a bad person or a bad wife or a bad mother. It also helped her to see that she had a family history of these kinds of problems and that she had the opportunity to break the pattern for her own children.

Dr. Weinstrand had Ray come to their third meeting to discuss some of the same things he had mentioned to Sheila. He also talked about the way in which Ray's anger and frustration, as well as his pain, could impact Sheila's recovery. When someone suffers from depression or bipolar disorder, it inevitably is an injury to his or her partner as well. However, if the partner reacts with intense emotional expression, it can sometimes add to the difficulties.

While it can be very difficult, at times, not to react to emotional provocation coming from the emotional volatility of a person with bipolar disorder, it is much more effective to respond calmly, out of an Adult ego state. Dr. Weinstrand talked with Ray about trying to use Stop, Drop, and Roll to intervene when he felt like he was about to respond to Sheila with anger. If Ray could Stop, then he would have a chance to think about how he was going to respond, or Drop. When Ray was able do this, his Roll step turned out to be a gentle stating of his needs and wants. Ray could see, very quickly, that as he practiced Stop, Drop and Roll with his response to Sheila he was much more effective when she was upset.

The process of helping people find a path through these kinds of difficult emotions, without squelching them, is quite an art. Luckily for Ray and Sheila, Dr. Weinstrand was pretty talented at helping couples learn to respect each other's feelings while learning to express them with less force.

Over the next few months, Sheila's medication regime began to settle in and continued to be more helpful in giving her relief from her intense mood swings. The meetings with Dr. Weinstrand were also quite enlightening. Sheila learned more about herself and her emotional makeup. They looked at how she had been ignoring her own personal needs and emotions in her desire to be a good mother.

When Sheila explored her history with Dr. Weinstrand, they

realized that her mother had not been very emotionally present during Sheila's childhood and that this injury was impacting her life now. Sheila's mother had been overly involved in taking care of her own mother, who had been hospitalized for depression. Sheila had been holding a lot of anger for her mother's abandonment, which made it a lot more difficult for her to admit her own difficulties in dealing with the dependency needs of Sarah and Terry, her own children. Sheila realized that while her intentions of staying home as a full-time mother were good, the reality was that that level of dependency was too stressful for her.

Ray and Sheila talked with each other, as well as with Dr. Weinstrand, at great length about how to solve Sheila's difficulties with parenting full time. They discussed how to relieve her from some of her childcare duties and the possibility of Ray and Sheila both working part time. They eventually decided that this would compromise their income too significantly, so they tried to find some part-time day care so Sheila could begin to work from home part time.

Sheila began by reconnecting to some of her old accounts. As she did this, she realized how much she had missed feeling important and valued in the adult world of work. The transition to this new lifestyle was far from completely smooth, however, since a lot of guilt surfaced as she spent time away from her children. But once the new plan had been in place for a while, Sheila found that she was able to be more fully emotionally available to her kids. She didn't feel so resentful of their needs, since many of her needs were being met as well.

Over time in therapy, Sheila learned to express her needs more regularly. She had been locked into a "Good" Kid mode, and all of her repressed feelings had erupted in a combination of depression and irritable mania. As she was able to understand her own emotions and work at expressing them assertively, she settled into a positive family and work lifestyle. She didn't sink into deep depressions. In addition, her explosive anger was a much less significant factor. She would still blow up briefly at times, but the explosions were less frequent and shorter lasting, with milder levels of expressed anger. Her new abilities in communication helped the marriage as well. Ray and Sheila found, with the help that Dr. Weinstrand gave them, that they were much better at connecting emotionally.

After a year in therapy, Dr. Weinstrand suggested that they didn't have to continue meeting regularly, since things seemed to be going well. They agreed that Sheila and Ray were welcome to come back if things started to go downhill. They planned on a six-month check-in session to make sure of that.

After another year of positive experiences, Sheila talked with Dr. Steinberg about reducing her medication regime. Gradually, they eliminated the antidepressant, with no ill effects. Eventually, she tried to go off of her mood stabilizer as well. This didn't work quite as effectively. After two weeks off of all of her medications, her irritability was beginning to increase again. She was getting more irritable with both Ray and the kids. When she met again with Dr. Steinberg, they agreed that she should stay on a low level of mood stabilizer to ensure that her moods didn't begin cycling dramatically again. Eventually, Sheila met only once every six months for fifteen minutes with Dr. Steinberg to make sure that her life continued to go well.

Sheila's case is not unusual, but a few issues should be noted here. Much more serious levels of bipolar disorder require much more intensive interventions. In addition to medication, frequently it's very important to recognize the impact of these problems on the people that care about the "identified patient," the one with the bipolar diagnosis. The anger of the bipolar person is frequently acted out in ways that damage their relationships with others, causing more depression and difficulty. The anger of significant others at the difficult behaviors engaged in by the person suffering from bipolar disorder can exacerbate the situation if those involved don't participate in family therapy or some appropriate intervention.

This same dynamic is found frequently with major depression. It is not unusual to find the partner of someone who is depressed also getting depressed, since the injury of having a partner who is injured can generate anger that gets turned into depression. The same principle of recognizing, understanding, and learning to effectively use anger—as well as the other emotions involved—is still central to psychotherapy with mood disorders.

The anger involved can relate to the genetic injury of irritability that accompanies bipolar disorder or major depression, injuries relating to childhood issues, and/or the injuries connected to events in adulthood and everyday life. If you have a major depression, like Simon did after his marriage fell apart, and you're dealing with the injury of divorce and abandonment that resonates with childhood issues, you need to be able to use the Stop, Drop, and Roll system to turn your anger out of depression and into assertive behavior and empowerment. You may need medication as well.

If you have a bipolar disorder, like Sheila, in addition to medication you will need to work on addressing the here-and-now injuries in your life by turning the anger energy into personal power. You need to take action, whatever that may mean for you. You may need to work with Stop, Drop, and Roll to help reduce your emotional volatility. Your partner may need to use Stop, Drop, and Roll to help them deal with their injuries about the disorder and to use their anger to work with you toward recovery while avoiding the escalation of conflict. Regardless of whether the mood disorder is bipolar disorder or major depression, understanding and utilizing the anger involved is essential to recovery.

# CHAPTER 6

# Anger and Addictions

## *"Please Love Me!"*

BECAUSE LIFE IS HARD, IT ISN'T SURPRISING THAT WE feel a need to escape from the struggles of our daily lives. All of us would like to feel good and to feel less pain and fear. In fact, we need to be able to conduct our lives in ways that take care of us and lead us to live in less pain and fear. The problem, though, is that people can get caught in behaviors that, at the time, seem to take care of them, but actually destroy the quality of their lives. These self-destructive behaviors make these people more comfortable, emotionally, in the short term—but in the long term, the same behaviors can distort and ruin their lives, as well as damage the lives of those close to them.

Addiction falls into this category of behaviors that seem to solve short-term problems but are self-destructive in the long term. Addictions are psychologically complicated sets of behaviors that simultaneously soothe and torment us. They are behaviors that involve repetitively abusing substances, usually alcohol or drugs, but also food or laxatives or another substance. In addition, an individual can be addicted to activities such as work, cleaning, exercise, or sex. What's more, the individual can become addicted to using substances or activities either too frequently or not frequently enough. But no matter what form it takes, all of these behaviors make the person feel better right now or feel less anxiety or pain right now.

Generally, when we are engaging in behaviors that attend to what is causing us pain, we are using the energy of anger. With addictions, we have learned how to stop the pain we might be feeling in the short term but not really fix the long-term injuries that lie underneath. This means that in addictions, the energy of anger is being used in a dysfunctional way. Unfortunately, using anger in a dysfunctional manner only causes more injury, which frequently turns the anger into guilt about misbehaving in some way.

In addictions, dysfunctional anger is caught in a guilt cycle that continues and increases the injuries. We feel bad and then use the addiction or dysfunctional anger to escape our bad feelings. Then we must face our guilt for behaving badly and because we feel bad we start the addictive cycle again. Quite simply, the anger isn't used to heal the injury.

Because there is so much injury in life, almost everyone has some sort of dysfunctional anger and some sort of addictive behavior. Beyond alcohol, drugs, and food, you can be addicted to television, video games, surfing the Internet, or pornography. There really are an almost infinite number of addiction behaviors, and you don't have to be totally addicted to abuse substances. You are abusing if you are using for emotional reasons and it is negatively impacting your life.

Like every aspect of mental health, addictions are a matter of degree. Dysfunction is relative and usually appears when things get extreme. Another way of understanding this would be to use a concept from statistics. The bell curve, or normal distribution, (see Figure 2) shows the way in which data tend to collect around the mean, which is the average. Most of the scores are close to the average score, and it is unusual to have scores that are out toward either end of the curve.

We begin to find dysfunction as people approach the ends, in either direction, of the normal or bell-shaped curve. This tends to be true on different mental health variables. As you get further and further away from the midpoint, you begin to find more and more dysfunction. An example of this would be to look at eating. People eat in many different ways, but at one end of the spectrum we would find people who seriously under eat. On the other end would be those who seriously overeat.

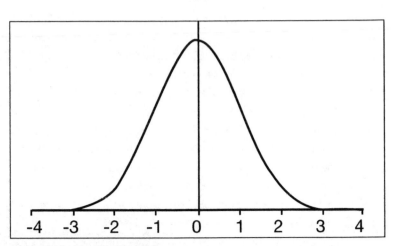

*Figure 2: The Normal Distribution*

## Childhood Roots of Addiction

Feeling good right now is a very poor substitute for being and feeling loved. Feeling less pain or fear right now are also very poor substitutes. However, many people grow up in ways that teach them that they cannot count on having another person love them. Even when they are in a committed relationship with someone who truly does love them, and whom they love, they may be unable to receive the love that is given. It is one thing to be loved and quite another to be able to allow yourself to receive those feelings.

So, how can someone become unable to receive love? The answer, typically, goes back to childhood experiences. When someone is sufficiently emotionally injured in trying to receive love from a parent, they learn to back away. They learn to be in retreat from other people, not to trust others, and not to pursue love. The way they retreat can vary. They may be *narcissistically retreated*, where they can only take care of themselves. They may be *depressively retreated*, where they learn to give up on being loved. Or they may be *masochistically retreated* into the "Good" Kid, where they are only able to take care of others in the frequently unfulfilled hope that someone will eventually recognize their sacrifice and come and love them back.

The *addictive retreat* is a form of narcissistic retreat, except that the retreat is into something that makes you almost feel loved. It is a retreat into something that makes you feel better right now without the risk of really counting on another person. The retreat never really works because no matter how valid our reasons are for retreating, the "Bad" Kid in us knows that we still need and deserve to be loved. We will continue to try to find ways to be loved, whether the methods are functional or dysfunctional. Trying to be loved is a use of anger. When the anger is being used to support an addictive process, it is dysfunctional. It doesn't bring us the love we really need and want.

Addictions almost always have some component of child-hood injury supporting this dysfunctional use of anger. It may be having had cold, distant parents who were depressed or emotion-ally unavailable. It may be having had alcoholic parents who raised you in a family context of rage and chaos. Regardless of the injuries back there, having a good understanding of them can help to put your addiction into perspective. In short-term work, you can use Stop, Drop, and Roll to take the angry energy that goes into cravings and redirect it toward healthy behaviors. In longer-term psychotherapy, you can use the very same angry energy that has supported the addiction to resolve and heal those injuries.

## The Emotional Dynamics of Addiction

Since addictive behaviors make us feel better, they elicit feelings that are similar to how we feel when we are being loved. However, this feeling of being loved is a deception. Addictive behaviors are as devoid of true love as candy is empty of true nutritional value.

For example, an alcoholic usually feels less pain and fear when he's had a few drinks. Frequently people use drugs and/or alcohol to escape the mundane everyday world that they live in. For these people, the here-and-now injury could be the monotony of their lives. The boredom that they experience would be a form of the anger that they feel in response to that injury. The dysfunction is to fall into a pattern of heavy use of alcohol instead of using the anger to find healthy ways to make their lives more interesting and fulfilling.

In terms of their basic emotional dynamics, there isn't much difference between addictions. Addictive behavior—whether it's overeating or under eating or drinking too much or spending far too much money or wasting time on the Internet—is based on deprivation of love and a misguided pursuit of love. One difference that I must point out, though, is that chemical addictions—addiction to drugs or alcohol—can become primary in their impact, in that they become the first thing that must be dealt with before any other healing can take place. They also can become self-perpetuating very quickly. They can produce symptoms that mimic more serious mental illnesses, causing delusions and hallucinations as well as bizarre behavior. This means that chemically based addictive behaviors are simultaneously a form of self-medication and symptom production. This adds a level of threat to chemical addictions.

The "Good" Kid and "Bad" Kid can both be involved in addictions, although in different ways. "Good" Kids and "Bad" Kids who have addictions are both attempting to find love. Both are using their anger, related to injuries in their past, to act on the world in an attempt to find the love that was lacking. "Good" Kids pursue the love of others, while "Bad" Kids are more focused on self-love, partly as a result of having learned that receiving the love of others is impossible. In the process of seeking love, the "Good" Kid is over controlled and the "Bad" Kid is under controlled. Tragically, neither strategy will lead them to gain the love they are seeking. While this misguided use of their anger provides some immediate positive feelings, it ends in isolation and shame. The bent anger of addiction ends in dysfunction, not in love.

"Bad" Kids tend to express their anger either outwardly, in antisocial activities or in some manner that shows rebellion. If you are more into your "Bad" Kid, your problems are more likely to include the expression of anger by engaging in "bad" behaviors such as promiscuity, drinking abusively, and/or using drugs illegally or inappropriately.

"Good" Kids, in contrast, have more inwardly focused anger. Their fears are exaggerated by their anger, and they end up locking in on some behavior that they've learned helps to reduce their anxiety. They tend to hide their problematic behaviors to avoid disapproval. The "Good" Kid may be overly involved in behaviors they expect to be pleasing to others. They abuse themselves, whether they are aware of it or not.

"Good" Kid addictions frequently include things like throwing up after eating what they consider to be too much or seriously under eating. People who use under eating as an addictive behavior are frequently pursuing external approval for their appearance. They may have distorted self-images. They may be anorexic and starving themselves but they look in the mirror and see themselves as obese. They fear being obese and avoiding eating relieves their anxiety. They are so concerned with pleasing other people and being "Good" Kids that they may starve themselves to death to avoid being seen as fat. Sometimes, too, there is a covert "Bad" Kid agenda, which is about punishing parents in a dysfunctional family system by hurting themselves.

Of course, most people will have some aspects of both "Good" Kid and "Bad" Kid dynamics functioning within them. Almost all problems in mental health involve matters of degree. Eating behaviors are an example where both the "Good" Kid and "Bad" Kid can exert influence to differing degrees. Eating behaviors are quite complex. People who use overeating are frequently coming from the "Bad" Kid position in terms of their eating. "Bad" Kids get to act out their anger and overeating can be a way to do just that. "Bad" Kid overeating is where the person feels entitled to get their emotional needs met through food, when it becomes an addictive substance that provides the feeling of love and nurturance. The passive-aggressive anger piece is present as well: "You can't make me stop eating!" However, they feel "bad" and guilty when they overindulge, which is evidence of the "Good" Kid being present.

With so many powerful feelings involved in addictions, it is easy to see how people can get addicted to all sorts of things. And you're right if you think that no one can really find love in a bottle of alcohol—but another drink might help you feel less pain or anxiety right now. No one can find love from cocaine, heroin, or other drugs, but usually they will help you to feel less pain right now. If you are obese, eating a quart of chocolate ice cream is an angry thing to do to yourself, but it will taste good with every bite, and in the short term it might make you feel better or less anxious right now. What will help in the long-term is to learn how to direct one's anger into nurturing and empowerment.

## Anger and Addiction

All addictive behaviors represent misguided anger. They are responses to the injury of not having received the love you needed in the past as well as the current injuries of everyday life. Instead of using the energy of anger to address these injuries, it is spent in the pursuit of things that make you feel good or less pain right now. There is nothing wrong with most of these behaviors when pursued in moderation. However, these short-term pleasures, when pursued to the extent of addiction, represent angry energy that has moved into dysfunction.

Our "Good" Kids tend to prevent us from pleasing ourselves while the "Bad" Kids rebel and demand gratification. Underneath, the Bad Parent voice criticizes us for attempting to meet our own needs.

Addiction, like depression, is a form of anger that is bent. Depression is easier to see, especially when we have depressive thoughts like "I don't deserve a good life." In addiction, the thought might be "I do deserve a quart of chocolate ice cream"—when you are obese and have health problems. This voice seems to be caring and nurturing but it's encouraging you to harm yourself.

Since addiction is a form of bent anger, we can use the Stop,

Drop, and Roll system to intervene and unbend the anger of addiction into healthy behaviors. In using Stop, Drop, and Roll with addictions, as always, the first step is to notice that you're on fire and Stop. If you don't notice the fire, you won't have a chance to address it. What this means for addictions is noticing the cravings, thoughts, or feelings that lead to addictive behavior.

For example, pushing yourself too hard at work may be the beginning of feeling like you really need a drink when you're through for the day. Or, seeing an advertisement for chocolate ice cream may lead you to buy it, which in turn will lead to eating it in a weak moment.

Once you've been able to notice the cravings and Stop, the next step would be to Drop. This means taking time to think about why these cravings are appearing now. What started the cravings in the here and now? How do these cravings resonate with injuries from your past?

Once the cravings are understood, the Roll step requires figuring out what you need to do with that anger instead of allowing it to go into the same old addictive pattern. What do you really need to take care of those injuries, past or present, instead of abusing yourself with the angry, addictive behavior? The Good Parent inside of you needs to use that caretaking behavior, in some way, to address the needs of the Hurt Child. Once this pattern is established, the addictive cycle is broken.

## Overcoming Roadblocks

To change addictive behavior, its anger-related energy needs to be redirected into empowerment and healing, and the Stop, Drop, and Roll steps can help. Unfortunately, roadblocks exist. These roadblocks include deprivation, overindulgence, and denial. In addition, the level of addiction can make healing even more difficult. Chemical addictions can take on a life of their own and require intervention to break out of a cycle that is damaging your ability to think clearly. Once you have the space to think, you can utilize the steps to unbend the anger in your system.

Despite these problems, addictions—and their roadblocks—can be overcome.

Deprivation is one common obstacle. You may think that a person with an addiction can simply remove from her life the substance or behavior that is causing her so much grief. You may think, "Why doesn't she just dump the liquor or drugs down the sink and avoid going to bars?"

Sometimes, for some people, deprivation does work, but this is the exception rather than the rule. Deprivation usually makes people feel pain and feel as if they aren't being loved. It can elicit old feelings of abandonment from childhood. Knowing that you can't have that next drink or line of cocaine can make you feel despair—and feel an increased need to have what's out of reach. The current injuries of withdrawal and/or cravings for whatever the desired object is resonates with those early childhood feelings of injury, lack of love, and abandonment. This resonance can make letting go of addictive behaviors extremely difficult for many people.

On the other hand, overindulgence is equally self-destructive and represents another obstacle to healing. Overindulgence of alcohol and/or cocaine, for example, leads to all of the negative events and feelings that follow a binge: being hung over, tired, and irritable, regretting the loss of money and perhaps the inappropriate behavior that you were involved in while intoxicated. In addition, while overindulgence allows people to escape their pain in the short term, it only returns later, multiplied. It returns because none of the underlying injuries has been addressed by the appropriate use of anger.

Plus, there are now the new injuries to deal with, such as problems with the law, in one's relationship, or at work. The ongoing pursuit of escape with drugs and/or alcohol generally leads to a steadily deteriorating quality of life. Addicted people, over time, frequently lose their most important relationships and support system.

In contrast to deprivation and over indulgence, empowerment works. Empowerment may involve the exact same behaviors as deprivation or even indulgence at times. However, the behavior will be different in that it will not be emotionally based. When we are empowered, we are choosing to change that behavior because it makes us feel more fulfilled. For example, if you are overweight, the dysfunctional use of your anger would be to feel guilty and beat yourself up after you eat. You can make yourself feel so terrible that you don't know what to do. Likely you'll go and eat the gallon of chocolate ice cream that you bought "for the kids" because you know that you can make yourself feel better in the short term with a quick dose of chocolate and sugar.

However, if you're able to Stop, Drop, and Roll when you notice the cravings, you may be able to put that same angry energy into going for a walk or a bike ride. Putting the anger into something that truly nurtures you—whether it's exercise, asking your partner for a hug, or giving yourself some time to relax—is more empowering than putting the anger into addictive self-abuse.

Unfortunately, people who are pursuing love through addictive behaviors usually don't understand what they are doing. They may not consciously feel deprived of love. They are likely to dismiss the damage that they received in growing up. They may even feel that they are empowered in their lives and point to their excessive self-restraint or indulgence without seeing it as unhealthy behavior. But, frequently, these individuals are in denial, a concept that is central to addiction.

According to the dictionary, *denial* is the repudiation or invalidation of something. In psychology, denial is a defense mechanism used unconsciously to avoid something unpleasant or painful. In addictions, denial is the process individuals go through to avoid the painful realization that what they are doing with whatever substance they are addicted to is causing them a great deal of pain. Denial, then, in addictions, is the opposite of making the problem conscious. It is the process of pushing unpleasant realities out of your consciousness.

And without being fully and deeply aware that you are abusing yourself with certain behaviors and paying attention to what you are doing, you will continue to act them out. For most people, addictive behaviors are very difficult to change, even when you are aware of them. It takes an extremely high level of awareness to know why and how you feel unloved.

Denial can take many forms. The classic is to insist that the problem is not a problem. Or you can just deny that it bothers you. "I'm not that heavy." "I don't drink any more than my friends." Denial never works, but it may buy you some time if you are a really good talker. You might convince yourself as well as others, on a certain level, that you aren't in trouble, but it won't change the reality of your problem.

Another example of denial is when an addict will dismiss his problematic childhood by pointing to others who have had worse experiences but are quite healthy adults. The addict points to these examples as a way of insisting that he should not have to sort through his long-lasting injuries. Fortunately or unfortunately, part of realizing that his life isn't working requires that he understands his emotional injuries. This understanding may allow him to make the changes that he deserves and requires.

Denial doesn't work. It can only postpone things. If you postpone some addictive behaviors long enough, you can die. Over indulgence doesn't work and deprivation doesn't work. What does work is learning to understand your injuries related to being loved, both past and present, and learning to use the accompanying anger in ways that are healthy and functional.

## Alcohol and Other Chemical Substances

Part of what makes dealing with addiction so difficult is that there are so many different dynamics and factors involved in the different behaviors. I'd like to devote a section to alcohol and drug addiction, since it is such a tremendous problem, one that affects more than twenty million people in the United States alone. Additionally, there are many dynamics related to alcohol that can be applied to other addictive behaviors such as gambling or overeating.

The social costs of chemical addiction are incredibly high. The National Institute on Drug Abuse did a national study in 1992 that was updated in 1995 on the total costs of alcohol and drug abuse, including medical costs, premature deaths, decreased productivity, motor vehicle crashes, crime, and social welfare cost estimates. The costs increased 12.5 percent over that three-year time span to an estimate of $276.3 billion. If you use the same projections today, it would likely be in the $400-500 billion range.

With alcohol addiction, there is evidence that some people have a genetic vulnerability; approximately two-thirds of that genetic vulnerability is physiological. In addition, there are also the "emotional" genetics, meaning that because of the emotional problems and substance abuse of the parents, the child is injured and more vulnerable to substance abuse. Those who become alcohol dependent—those who are physiologically addicted—frequently have a family history of alcoholism. Other environmental risk factors include alcohol-abusing peers during adolescence, although this is also a common problem for adults who are alcoholic.

Another complication is differentiating between *alcohol abuse* and *alcohol dependency*. Those who abuse alcohol frequently behave in a very similar manner to those who are alcohol dependent, in terms of the amount of alcohol consumed and their lifestyle. But those who are alcohol dependent—those who are physiologically dependent on alcohol—have alcohol as the centrally organizing aspect of their lives. There is compulsivity about its use and an inability to stop or control one's drinking, even when the desire to do so is present.

There are three symptoms that signal that an individual is becoming physiologically addicted to alcohol and is alcohol dependent.

One is to look at one's tolerance for alcohol, either noticing that it takes a significantly increasing amount of alcohol to achieve intoxication or that there is a decreased effect from drinking the same amount of alcohol. While it is possible to develop tolerance without being addicted, it is a serious warning sign.

The second symptom of alcohol dependency is daily versus less frequent drinking. Abusive drinkers may go for a number of days, or sometimes even weeks, without drinking. If there is never a day that goes by without a drink you are likely, but not necessarily, physiologically dependent on alcohol.

Related to daily usage is the fact that people who suffer from substance dependency find that they are drawn to using increasingly larger amounts for a longer time than they had intended. Getting and using the substance takes up a larger chunk of their life and consciousness. Those who are alcohol dependent will attempt to cut down their usage and find that they are unsuccessful and that alcohol begins to impact their lives in significant and detrimental ways. But even when they recognize this negative impact, they still find themselves unable to change their behavior.

Finally, if there are any signs of withdrawal from alcohol, the individual is physiologically dependent, though it is possible to be dependent without experiencing withdrawal. Symptoms of withdrawal can begin within as little as a few hours and certainly within twelve hours. It is more likely that withdrawal symptoms will appear within a day or two. In my experience, most who are physiologically dependent on alcohol will begin to experience some signs of withdrawal within six to forty-eight hours. Of course, most people who are addicted to alcohol, as opposed to abusive drinkers, will not go three days without using.

Some of the withdrawal symptoms are relatively minor, like increased sweating, breathing, and heart rate, or being flushed, jittery, anxious, irritable, or agitated. It is not unusual for people in withdrawal to experience difficulty in sleeping, sometimes to the point of insomnia, and their hands may begin to shake more than usual.

But there are more serious and threatening symptoms, including nausea and vomiting. Many people have heard of the "shakes" or the "DT's," which stands for Delirium Tremens. This refers to a state where the person in withdrawal is experiencing auditory, visual, or tactile hallucinations and they are psychotic (they are out of touch with reality). There are many stories about people feeling as though there are bugs crawling all over their bodies. Delirium Tremens generally begin at two to seven days of abstinence, and can have up to a 40 percent mortality rate if untreated. Usually patients suffering from DT's have an underlying medical illness.

Also of great concern is the possibility of experiencing what are called grand mal seizures, a temporary, overall short-circuiting of the brain. These seizures are most often associated with epilepsy, but can be experienced with other medical problems as well. Seizures can be induced, though rarely, by alcohol withdrawal. When someone experiences a grand mal seizure, they are at risk for experiencing convulsions and can even die from the experience.

Since there are so many potentially serious difficulties involved in alcohol withdrawal, as well as withdrawal from opiates or sedatives, I recommend that anyone who believes that they may be at risk contact a physician as well as a trained addictions psychotherapist. Physicians can prescribe medications to help to ensure that withdrawal is safer and less difficult. A medically supervised withdrawal may also help reduce the difficulties with future withdrawals as well. Some people can only withdraw from alcohol safely in some supervised context, where medical and psychological help is always available. This would be in a hospital in-patient setting, or in either an in-patient or daily-contact, intensive outpatient alcohol and drug treatment program.

You may notice that I've begun to talk about "substance" problems and not just alcohol. That is because most people who are dependent on or abusing alcohol are frequently using and/or abusing other drugs. They may have more than one dependency or they may simply use the other drugs while high on alcohol. Either scenario can and does happen with considerable frequency.

Besides alcohol, people can be physiologically addicted to

heroin and all of the other opiates. There are quite a number of prescription opiates that are physiologically addicting. Additionally, all of the benzodiazepines, the group of minor tranquilizers, can be physiologically addicting. Usage of all of these drugs may require withdrawal, with different levels of severity. Withdrawal from tranquilizers is likely to cause a marked increase in anxiety levels, but is usually not physically threatening.

People may also be emotionally addicted to other substances such as marijuana or cocaine. Even though these addictions may be quite severe and problematic, these substances have not been found to be physiologically addictive. People withdrawing from them may suffer some physiologic responses, and while those can be quite difficult, they are usually emotionally based. The same can be said about other emotionally addictive behaviors such as gambling, sex, and eating.

It's important to note that it isn't unusual for drug and alcohol abusers to have other diagnoses. This is what's called *dual diagnosis*. People who are depressed, bipolar, or suffering from any number of anxiety conditions may turn to drugs and/or alcohol in an attempt to self-medicate these underlying problems. They may even turn to the non-chemical addictions.

But more effective and less physiologically and psychologically destructive medications are available for you from an appropriate physician. Whatever drug or condition you may be struggling with, I would recommend a consultation with your family physician and an addiction specialist before you begin to withdraw.

While many people believe that people suffering from alcohol and/or drug problems cannot be treated successfully, the reality is that the great majority can. As much as sixty-five percent of the people who go through a first-time alcohol treatment program are able to maintain their sobriety after one year. This percentage is markedly higher when an addiction psychotherapist is seen weekly for a year following the treatment program. Of course, there are many who require further treatment programs, and many people are very resistant to treatment. Alcoholics often refer to "hitting bottom" as a description for reaching the point in their lives when they are willing to do whatever it takes to remain sober. Unfortunately, there are some who never find their "bottom" before they die.

A central aspect of alcohol and drug abuse is that, in addition to impacting the life functioning of the person who is suffering, it also damages the lives of the people they are most close to. If the abuser doesn't get help, eventually they will lose their important relationships. Their support system disappears. It impacts them occupationally as well as socially. They lose their jobs. It impacts their health. As with any major mental health problem, it impacts their entire life.

There are many instances of abuse of children in families with one or more parents suffering from drug and alcohol problems. The abuse is often in the form of neglecting their children as well as their spouses. Unfortunately, the abuse is also frequently active and can be physical and even sexual in nature. This takes the problems of the person suffering from the addiction and spreads it throughout their immediate family. Many children of alcohol and drug abusers suffer from various forms of mood and anxiety disorders and are vulnerable to relationship problems throughout their adult lives.

Alcohol can be incredibly destructive when it grows into abuse or dependency. Anger is involved in addiction in the dysfunctional behaviors of the addiction process itself. The repeated behavior of alcohol abuse is anger that is not being directed to really fix what is hurting you. Alcohol also is frequently associated with both interpersonally abusive behaviors on the part of the drinker as well as passive-aggressive behaviors such as not showing up for commitments and breaking agreements. Passive-aggression draws anger toward you. Denial is a form of passive-aggression in that it disputes the obvious reality of your self-destruction. This both injures and angers your significant others. Certainly people in withdrawal are more irritable or angry than they normally are. Stop, Drop, and Roll can play a significant role in helping to refocus and make the anger functional in any of these contexts.

## Bruce's Story

Bruce's story presents us with an opportunity to look at someone who redirected his anger and conquered his alcohol addiction. Bruce was a forty-year-old successful business owner who had started a software company with a couple of guys that he'd known while working as an engineer at a larger corporation. They had seen an opportunity and had found a very lucrative niche providing a service to the larger corporation.

Bruce and his partners, Joe and Mark, all enjoyed drinking quite a bit. They had, in fact, formed the idea for the company while at a bar, over drinks. But they didn't merely enjoy drinking—they all had problems with alcohol. Joe, Mark, and Bruce were out drinking almost every night. Frequently they'd even get started at lunch. Many days, their lunches would last into the evening. In this they were typical of alcohol abusers, who tend to surround themselves with people who drink too much. This makes their behavior seem socially acceptable.

Bruce was happily married with two young sons. His wife, Margaret, worked as an events planner for another large corporation, which was how she and Bruce had met. Margaret didn't really approve of Bruce's drinking. When Bruce was intoxicated, he would become more irritable and at times he would go into rages. Margaret was particularly concerned when Bruce upset the boys with his yelling and screaming. The boys would get really fearful when this was going on. It was Margaret's insistence that brought Bruce into treatment. After the last fight, she'd told him to get his drinking under control or she was going to divorce him.

When I met Bruce, he was very stressed out. His business had grown to more than forty employees and the company was doing very well. But problems lurked under the surface. Bruce felt very concerned for his employees. Bruce and his partners had borrowed a significant amount of money to get the business started and then had to borrow more as it expanded. While the business was doing well, it needed to continue to grow. If it didn't, there would be a time when those debts came due and they wouldn't be able to make the payments.

Bruce was the president of the company and its most visible spokesperson. He felt responsible for all of his employees and the success of the company. At times he felt like he had a tiger by the tail. He had to keep finding food or it would turn on him.

Bruce had grown up in rural upstate New York. His father was physically and emotionally abusive and drank a lot. His mother was the glue that held their large farming family together. They were fairly poor, and his mother had to work as a teacher to support the family. She'd gone to college, while his father had not.

Bruce was smart and a good student, encouraged by his mother. His success in school turned out to be his ticket out of town when he won a college scholarship for engineering. Bruce had had problems with authority, however, as long as he could remember. In college, these problems continued, but he knew that he had to watch himself or he'd lose his scholarship. Bruce started drinking to relieve the pressure of all the resentment he felt about having to work so hard to keep up. He was able to maintain his grades by keeping his alcohol consumption down to weekends, when he would binge.

Later, after he'd graduated, got a job, and was out on his own, he drank regularly. Once Bruce had found a significant level of success, he felt entitled to drink whenever he pleased. Drinking was often a part of his business meetings, but it had gotten more and more out of control. Bruce found himself drinking on his own at home.

When he first met Margaret, she'd gone along with the partying and the drinking. However, after they were married, and especially after they had kids, Margaret grew more concerned. She noticed that Bruce was drinking more and more and that his moods got worse and worse. He always seemed to be blowing up at someone. It seemed like almost anytime someone disagreed with him it would set him off. He just couldn't tolerate anything not working the way he needed it to work.

When Bruce started treatment with me, I was most concerned with getting his drinking under control. I recommended that he stop for a while and see how it felt to him. I also recommended that he start attending Alcoholics Anonymous. At first, Bruce cooperated by cutting down his drinking. He didn't want to attend AA meetings. He thought he was doing really well at keeping it under control. He didn't think his problem was that much of a problem. He was still in denial.

Bruce's sense of being in control of his drinking lasted about two weeks. He had gone to another business luncheon with his partners and ended up getting totally drunk. When he got home that evening, he was loud and argumentative with Margaret, who confronted him. After this latest disaster, he decided to stop drinking completely. Bruce was lucky in that he was able to stop without any signs of withdrawal. He even went to a couple of AA meetings, but felt that he just didn't fit in. I tried to encourage him to attend some other meetings, but he refused. He had trouble with the higher power issue.

Several weeks after Bruce stopped drinking he became extremely anxious. He suffered through several panic attacks before I could get him in to see a psychiatrist. When he met with the psychiatrist, they decided that Bruce had a bipolar mood disorder. Bruce had a dual diagnosis of alcohol abuse on top of a bipolar mood disorder. The psychiatrist felt that Bruce had been attempting to self-medicate his mood problem with alcohol. His psychiatrist put him on a mood stabilizer, which helped his anxiety a great deal. He also used some tranquilizers sparingly.

Over time, however, Bruce found that changing his lifestyle was quite painful. Bruce found that he was stable now, but he was kind of depressed. He felt embarrassed to be out and not drinking. His partners still drank way too much, and it wasn't easy to be around them—and he had to be around them a lot.

I urged him to discuss this with his psychiatrist. When he

did, they decided to add in an antidepressant medication, which helped him to be stable without being depressed or anxious most of the time.

Bruce's anger with his father took quite a while to get to in therapy. He was resistant to looking at those hurts and angers. His father had embarrassed him a great deal as a child, publicly humiliating him on a number of occasions. When we were able to access and work through his anger with his father, he found it became easier for him to deal more effectively with his partners. If they wanted to drink, he didn't really enjoy being around them, but he could handle it as long as they didn't get really obnoxious. When that would happen, he would just leave.

After about three years of sobriety, Bruce decided to see if he could handle social drinking. He started out by trying to have wine with dinner. But he gradually drank more and more and eventually ended up drinking heavily and drinking alone. When he finally told me about his experiment, I discussed the ways in which alcohol would mess up the balance of his medications. If you have a history of drinking heavily, you train your liver and kidneys to dump the alcohol quickly from your body. When you start to drink alcohol again, your liver and kidneys quickly clean the medications out of your body, along with the alcohol. This causes emotional instability.

I also asked him to talk to his psychiatrist about it. They decided that he could use Antabuse to get the distance he needed from alcohol and get stabilized again on his medications. Antabuse is a medication you can take that makes you allergic to alcohol. You have to be able to be sober for at least one but preferably two days before you can take Antabuse.

Bruce was able to stay sober long enough to take Antabuse. He spent almost three months on it before he felt that he was able to maintain his distance from alcohol. He had learned his lesson. While some people can come away from alcohol abuse and return to social drinking, others cannot. Even though Bruce had not been physiologically addicted to alcohol, he found that once he started he could not control his drinking.

While Bruce was in treatment, we worked on his explosive anger using Stop, Drop, and Roll. We used that same technique to work on intervening with his cravings for alcohol. Eventually, as he worked through his anger with his father, Bruce was less irritable and explosive. His medications also helped a great deal to moderate his moods. Bruce was able to stay sober. He continued to take his medications and remained stable over the course of a year, at which time we decided to stop psychotherapy.

## The Case of Joan

Another client of mine, Joan, also struggled with alcohol, and her story is more typical than Bruce's in that she experienced a more intense roller-coaster of emotions and behaviors before she was able to conquer her addiction. Joan was forty-six years old when she came to see me. She was a marketing researcher and had been employed by a large corporation doing reports for their marketing department. She came in because she had lost her job and felt both anxious and depressed.

Joan was happily married to Gregory, who worked as a high school teacher. Gregory and Joan had no children. They both came from difficult family backgrounds and didn't want the stress of trying to raise a family.

Joan's family was especially difficult. Her father was an alcoholic and frequently came home drunk and angry. Joan's mother was very intimidated by her father and came across as inadequate and helpless. Joan was the middle of three daughters, and her oldest sister, Sally, committed suicide three years after she'd moved out of the family home. Joan had known, as did the entire family, that Sally had been really depressed. She'd left home, failed out of the college that she'd attended, and lost several jobs. Joan had never forgiven herself, or her parents, for not helping Sally. In fact, in many ways the family had never really dealt with the loss.

About a month into therapy, Joan began to show signs that she was drinking too much. She missed a couple of sessions and when she called to say she'd miss her second appointment, her voicemail message had significantly slurred speech and didn't really make sense.

At her next appointment I confronted her about her having missed the last two meetings as a result of being inebriated. This was a clear indication that she was having a problem with drinking. She denied that she had a problem and said that she wanted to continue to work on her problems with anxiety and depression.

Two weeks later, I received a page to her home phone number. It was Gregory, Joan's husband. He was very upset. He'd come home from work to find Joan drunk to the point of incoherency. She had made a big mess in the house and was out of control. She alternated between being combative and being extremely apologetic and tearful. He didn't know what to do with her and was worried that she'd hurt herself. I recommended that he take her to the local emergency room for evaluation and a possible in-patient stay.

At the emergency room, Joan was evaluated. Her blood alcohol level was 0.38, more than four times the legal limit for being under the influence. She was put on a seventy-two-hour hold, as she had been threatening suicide in the emergency room while being so highly intoxicated.

I visited Joan in the hospital the next day. She was more coherent and wanted very much to get out of the hospital, even though her breath still stank of alcohol and she still seemed to be somewhat intoxicated. I let her know that she would be much better served to get through the seventy-two hours of the hold to see if she was starting to be in a state of withdrawal. While Joan was quite resistant to the idea of staying another night, she did eventually listen to my recommendation with the support of her husband, Gregory. By the second day, she had sobered up and was more willing to listen to reason. She agreed that she had a problem with alcohol and promised to attend Alcoholics Anonymous as a condition of having her hold released a day early.

Joan did go to AA and even found that she liked many of the people in the meetings. Over the next few weeks, she continued to attend meetings and worked on applying for new jobs. We also explored some of her feelings of anger for her father and her family. We began to connect her fears about her unemployment to her unfinished grieving for her sister, Sally. Sally had failed out of college and struggled to maintain her employment. Joan's exaggerated fears about her own employment connected her to unfinished emotions related to her sister's difficulties and suicide.

However, six weeks after she had been released from the hospital, Joan began to repeat the same pattern. She started missing appointments. The second time she missed I phoned her at home to see why she was late. She answered and was obviously intoxicated. I confronted her about her drinking and she denied it to me while we were on the phone. At our next appointment, I asked Gregory to accompany Joan.

While in the session, I asked if they still kept alcohol in the house. Gregory said that they had decided not to keep any alcohol in the home. He said that he had found an empty bottle of hard liquor in the garbage after Joan had missed her last appointment. At this point, Joan admitted to buying the bottle. She said she thought that she would be able to have one or two drinks without getting out of control.

Joan was beginning to realize that she couldn't drink at all without drinking to the point of severe impairment. Two weeks later, after swearing that she would never drink again and returning to AA, Joan was hospitalized with a blood alcohol level of 0.43. After another two-day stay on the in-patient unit, Joan agreed to participate in the hospital's out-patient alcohol treatment program, an AA-based education-oriented treatment program that was supervised by a psychiatrist and staffed with highly skilled mental health workers and nurses. The six-week program ended with Joan leaving with a clear plan to maintain her sobriety.

Unfortunately, two months later, Joan was back in the hospital again. She hadn't been able to maintain her sobriety outside of the hospital. Additionally, she had missed a number of appointments with me again and had again lied to me about her drinking habits. After her three days in the hospital and several treatment plan meetings attended by Joan, Gregory, myself, and her in-patient treatment team, it was decided that she needed to change two aspects of her treatment plan.

One change entailed her admission to a twenty-eight-day residential treatment program. The other change was for her to find a new therapist. It was clear that she wasn't being honest with me about what she was doing outside of treatment. The treatment team thought that because of her negative transference dynamics with her father, it might be more effective for her to have a female therapist. I agreed to this since it was clear that she wasn't able to be honest with me. She hadn't been able to reach out to me or anyone else when she had been feeling the cravings to drink. We all agreed that if she couldn't share her fears and feelings with me, she wasn't going to be able to get the support she needed to remain sober.

Joan found that her month-long residential treatment program helped get her over the top. She found a female therapist with whom she did feel comfortable connecting when she was feeling vulnerable. The combination of AA, her therapist, and Gregory's support had been working. Last I'd heard, Joan had over seven months of sobriety and was doing well, though sobriety is never something you can take for granted. She'd also found new employment, which helped her self-esteem as well.

## A Few More Thoughts

Addictions, with or without substances, are very serious and difficult mental health problems. They can be life threatening. They can be dealt with effectively, however, once they are admitted to and treatment is sought. While not everyone finds it so easy to resolve their addictive problems, once they are owned they usually can be treated successfully.

Addictions, also, are dysfunctional expressions of anger. That anger relates to everything from the here-and-now normal life injuries that we all experience on a daily basis to injuries that have been unresolved from childhood. Stop, Drop, and Roll can help you to confront your cravings as you work to withdraw from these self-destructive uses of anger.

I would encourage anyone who thinks that they may have a problem to seek a consultation with a physician, an addictions specialist, and/or a mental health specialist. Frequently the hardest part is admitting to the problem. Then, you need to make a commitment to yourself and the people you love. That commitment is to use the underlying dysfunctional anger to empower you to do whatever it takes to recover and find fulfillment.

# CHAPTER 7

# Anger and Intimacy

## *"We Still Need the Eggs!"*

YOU'RE PROBABLY WONDERING WHY I INCLUDED THIS strange statement about eggs in the title of a chapter on intimacy. It's a reference to the old Woody Allen movie *Annie Hall*. In it, Woody tells his friend that he believes that there are two jokes that seem to summarize his experience with relationships.

The first is an old Groucho Marx joke, which goes: "I wouldn't want to be a member of a club that would have me as a member." This joke seems to illustrate much of what we see in the dating scene, where everyone's interested in someone who doesn't seem to be interested in them. It's almost like a daisy chain, where John likes Carol who likes David who likes Melanie, and so on and so on. One wonders how anyone ever finds a partner.

This joke illustrates how low self-esteem causes problems in relationships. Because I don't like myself, if someone else likes me, then they don't know anything. However, if they don't like me, then they must have a lot on the ball. If I could get their approval, it would prove that I'm OK. Ever hear the word *codependency*? That's a form of transference where we look almost entirely for our esteem from significant others. It is a way in which low self-esteem impacts relationships.

Woody Allen's second joke uses the chapter subtitle as its punch line. A man goes to a psychiatrist and says, "Doctor, doctor, you've got to help me! My brother thinks he's a chicken." The doctor responds, "Gee, that's terrible! Why don't you bring him in and we'll fix him up for you." The man says, "Doctor, we'd like to do that, but we can't." The doctor says, "Why not?" The man then responds, "We still need the eggs!"

In the movie, Woody Allen goes on to say that this is what relationships are like. They're frustrating and make you feel crazy because they don't seem to make sense, but you "still need the eggs," the emotional intimacy. You still need the caring of other people and the connection to them in spite of all the complications that come with relationships. You still need to care for other people as well.

In this chapter you will learn the definition of emotional intimacy and learn the importance of anger, as well as other emotions, to being successful in this incredibly important aspect of your life. The focus will be, to a great extent, on how conflict resolution is an opportunity for greater emotional closeness. The important roles in relationships played by the main ego states—Parent, Adult, and Child—will be explained. You'll also learn to use the Stop, Drop, and Roll system to give your relationship a clear framework for resolving conflicts and achieving greater closeness. The frequently present and difficult passive-aggressive/hostile-dependent dynamics of relationship anger will be explained as well.

## What's Intimacy?

To put intimacy into perspective, it is one of the three worlds of human interaction. The others are the world of work and the world of socialization. These three worlds constitute a continuum of relationships, with socialization sitting between work and intimacy. The world of work has relatively clear rules and lines of authority. Power and authority roles are usually defined, although this varies (at some jobs it seems no one's in charge). In the world of intimacy there are rules as well, but they aren't as clear as they are in the world of work, even if they are spelled out in marital pledges or contracts. The world of socialization has the fewest rules, outside of basic manners and the law of the land.

The dictionary defines intimacy as being close or familiar, having to do with love or sex, very personal, or private. This leaves a lot of room for interpretation about what intimacy is, but it doesn't really tell us much about how to be intimate with others.

To be emotionally intimate with another person, the primary requirement is that the two people agree to honor each other's emotions. *This does not mean that they have to like those emotions.* It means only that they agree to respect each other's intrinsic right to experience the emotions that they have. I emphasize this because the difficulty we have with feelings that we don't like in our partner tends to be the major source of couples' communication conflicts. Perhaps you can already begin to see why intimacy is the hardest thing to do in life, even though we all "still need the eggs."

While the first and most important aspect of emotional intimacy is a mutual respect for each other's feelings, sharing a sufficient number of goals and values are tied for second place. A couple must share enough goals and values for this fragile, invisible third entity, this "us," to exist. They don't need to be totally in tune on all of these issues, but some goals are not negotiable. For example, if one person wants to have children, while the other is completely against the idea, we have a real conflict that has the potential to end the relationship. Additionally, the couple needs to share enough interests to make the relationship viable. They don't need to share all of their interests, but enough so that they can have fun together.

In addition to honoring our partner's emotions and sharing interests, intimacy requires that we must also be in touch with our own emotions as well. One question must be answered over and over again throughout the course of the relationship: "When does it take care of me to take care of you, and when does it *not* take care of me to take care of you?" This central question of intimacy can only be answered if you are emotionally intimate with yourself. This means that you must be in touch with your own emotions before you can share them with someone else. Being in touch with your emotions is a skill, one that can be acquired even if it doesn't come naturally. This means you can do it if you practice paying attention to yourself emotionally (see Chapter Two).

## Anger and Intimacy

Anger plays a central role in emotional intimacy, mostly because it is such a difficult feeling for all of us. Also, because there is so much injury in relationships as well as in life, a lot of anger is generated. Since anger can be scary and threatening to both the person who is feeing it and to his or her partner, it is usually challenging to honor it. To be clear, honoring your partner's anger does not mean that one should accept anger that is expressed abusively, either actively or passively. There is a difference between expressing anger and being abusive with it.

Expressed anger is frequently the first step toward being able to recognize the injuries that underlie the anger of your partner. If you are able to show empathy for your partner's injury it can bring you closer together. In fact, one of the best responses you can give a partner when they appear to be angry is to ask, "What do you need right now?" It's amazing how that question cuts underneath the anger and goes directly to their injury, frequently defusing a conflict before it escalates.

The need to be able to address the underlying injury is why sharing your anger with your partner can be a gift. If you express it directly and non-abusively, it gives your partner intimate information about who you are. It can facilitate the empathic connection. Emotions, in many ways, are the most intimate aspect of who we are. Sharing any of your emotions is a gift, and, of course, we most like to receive the favorable emotions. However, if you don't share your hurts and anger, you will be more likely to hold that anger inside of you as resentment. Resentments will eventually surface, usually with greater force for having been withheld.

If you look closely, you'll see that withholding your anger is passive-aggressive. Since being emotionally intimate contains an implicit agreement to share your feelings with each other, hiding your anger—or any other important emotions—is a form of betrayal. The withholding can be expressed in many ways but it usually will injure the hostile-dependent partner and draw their anger toward you. This passive-aggressive/hostile-dependent dynamic is seen frequently in problematic relationships. Remember, anger is not just yelling and screaming.

There are many ways to express anger. Many of them do not fit what people think of as angry behavior, and many of them are destructive. Passive-aggression is cold and angry. Sarcasm and other forms of humor can carry a lot of destructive anger, though it is important to be able to be humorous in a non-angry, playful way. Putting someone down, even when it doesn't seem obvious, is another way to express destructive anger. Yelling and screaming are hot, but not necessarily destructive if they are just occasional outbursts. If it's not done abusively, it is an indication that there are problems that need to be addressed. It is abusive and destructive if you're yelling and screaming names at each other, however. In contrast, assertive behavior—asking for what you want—is a constructive use of your anger.

Anger permeates relationships because we all get injured so frequently, both in and out of relationships. Since being emotionally intimate requires accepting each other's feelings, we will be required to accept our partner's angry feelings when they surface. Also, our partners will have to accept the fact that we may be injured by their angry feelings. We may respond to their anger by getting injured and angry as well. This is what escalation is all about.

Fortunately, the very same angry energy that can be used destructively in relationships can also be use constructively. In intimacy, the energy of anger, just as in other areas, is meant to fix what is causing you pain and injury. Most people are in a relationship with someone they love and who loves them. Unfortunately, love doesn't preclude getting injured. In fact, many of us have chosen partners, as a result of transference dynamics from our childhoods, who duplicate some of the more injurious aspects of our families. We do this unconsciously, to try to use the anger that was unsafe to use to try to change our parents when we were little. In many ways, we create relationships that mimic the difficulties we had with our parents and then try to elicit change from our partners in the here and now.

Angry energy in relationships usually contains anger and injuries that relate to both our old and current intimate relationships. The challenge is how to use the anger to draw closer to the person you love instead of using it to push them away. That is the double bind of anger. We are angry because we, in some way, are not receiving the love that we want and need. That is the injury. The double bind is that if we don't use the anger to meet our needs, they won't be met; and, if we use it inappropriately, we can also not meet our needs. It seems like a lose/lose situation. The only path out of the double bind is to use that angry energy to bring us the love that we need so that everyone wins.


## Barriers to Intimacy

So, how do you use your anger to untangle the emotional knots of intimacy instead of tying more of them tighter and tighter? How do two people who start out so excited about each other so often end up distant and miserable?

The answer to this is complicated. There are as many different answers as there are different couples. However, some concepts and patterns hold true in general and can be helpful. Problems with dysfunctional uses of anger, as you'll see, are at the heart of most problems with intimacy.

The concept of transference—"old business"—comes into play here. What we learn from our parents about emotions and intimacy colors all of our subsequent relationships. I sometimes describe transference as similar to the experience of wearing glasses that have Coke-bottle bottoms for lenses. You still receive information visually, but it can be incredibly distorted and hard to understand. These distortions are a major part of the difficulty involved in miscommunication conflicts.

For example, a partner might hear statements twisted by

what they perceive to be sarcasm, when none was intended. They may be getting meta-communication, information in the form of a facial expression or tone of voice that has been misinterpreted. Meta-communications are the most easily distorted type of communication. However, even good old talking is susceptible to amazing levels of distortion. People frequently hear nonsense, or even the opposite of what is intended, just based on difficulties in hearing accurately.

Transference takes current experiences and magnifies or distorts them based on injuries from the past. Since most transference difficulties relate to injuries, the feelings that tend to get exaggerated are the emotions that follow an injury: sadness, fear, and anger. James, the young carpenter whose story we looked at in Chapter Two, is a good example of transference. He would explode in anger in response to being teased by coworkers, but his anger was exaggerated by his old injuries from his family, especially the ones he received from his older brother. These kinds of dynamics can go on in all relationships but are more likely to appear most intensively in our intimate relationships, since the old injuries occur in our most intimate relationships as a child.

Another concept related to intimacy is the idea of ego states, which I've already discussed in previous chapters. This concept was made famous in the 1970s by Eric Berne in his book *Games People Play*. I believe this idea continues to be quite helpful in understanding relationships. The basic concept is that each individual has (at least) three different ego states: Parent, Adult, and Child. When two people relate to each other, especially in the context of intimacy, all of the relationships between their ego states are important and come into play.

Generally, the most important of these relationships are the ones shown in the diagram with arrows. Those are the Child-Child relationship, the Adult-Adult interaction, the Parent-Parent dyad, and the two Parent-Child relationships. To have a truly effective relationship, all of these ego state relationships need to work successfully. The exception would be if a couple had no children; in that case, the Parent-Parent dynamic would be less important.

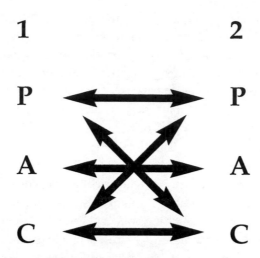

1  2

P ⟷ P

A ⤬ A

C ⟷ C

*Figure 3: Ego States and Relationship Dynamics*

A couple needs to have their Child ego states "play" well together in whatever context they both find rewarding. Play may be participating in anything that they enjoy, such as going to movies, playing sports, reading and discussing books, going to the theater, or playing cards or board games.

The Adult ego state relationship has a different dynamic. The partners need to meet effectively with their Adult ego states to fulfill their responsibilities, make life plans, and so on.

The Parent ego state relationship serves a different function. If the partners are raising children, they need to be able to sort out effective and unified strategies to do so, which means meeting in their Parent ego states.

While problems can exist in any of those ego state pairings, in my experience, the most problematic of the pairings, or dyads, are the two Parent-Child relationships. In those dyads, each Child ego state needs to receive Good Parenting from the other's Parent ego state.

## Max and Suzie's Story

Let's take a look at Max and Suzie to see how these concepts play out in a relationship. They're an attractive young couple. Max runs a small company that builds homes, and Suzie's a stewardess. Since they both have demanding schedules, and Suzie travels so frequently, they frequently missed their quality time together. They discussed the problem and agreed to have a quiet, romantic weekend together. However, Max's foundation subcontractor informed him that they could either pour the foundation of his new project that weekend or they would push it out another month. Max was unhappy about having to work on the weekend, but he needed to get the project going since all of his other subcontractors were scheduled to follow in the upcoming weeks. When he agreed to have the foundation poured, he'd forgotten about his weekend plans with Suzie.

When he discovered the conflict, he told Suzie. She became angry and accused him of never wanting to pay attention to her. He got defensive and "just tried to explain" the mistake. Suzie got quiet, walked into the other room, and picked up the phone. She began scheduling a work trip that would take her away for ten days. Max tried to talk her out of it, and when she didn't respond he told her to take a longer trip. When she didn't reply, he ended up telling her to not come back at all. Things escalated from there.

Max and Suzie's problem is an example of a typical communication conflict in which the injuries don't get addressed, aren't understood, and don't get resolved. The problem began with a miscommunication about scheduling. When the conflict became apparent, Suzie got injured and responded to Max with anger out of her Hurt Child ego state. This caused Max to be injured and go into his Hurt Child ego state. Max responded by becoming defensive. He didn't realize that Suzie was hurt; he only saw her passive-aggressive anger. When he attempted to connect with her, her anger and pain wouldn't allow her to respond, and then he became even more hurt. He struck out with anger out of his Hurt Child ego state, and serious escalation was under way. Although neither could have identified it, both Max and Suzie experienced each other as being in a Bad Parent ego state, rejecting and demanding.

In intimate relationships, partners usually hurt each other unintentionally, at least initially. Once someone's operating out of her Hurt Child ego state, it isn't unusual for her to strike—or strike back—in anger. This makes it appear as if she has the intention to hurt, much in the same way that communication distortions allow people to mishear and assume that the other intends to harm. Frequently, the exaggeration of these kinds of injuries is a function of transference dynamics, the distorting lens made out of childhood emotional injuries that can confound communication.

When we are in our Hurt Child, we frequently strike out at our loved ones with the anger that follows injury. It may be expressed from the hot end of the anger spectrum in yelling and screaming or from the cold end in passive-aggressive behavior. It may be spoken directly or appear as a sarcastic tone of voice. It may sneak out in hostile looks, facial expressions such as rolling one's eyes. It is unusual for someone in their Hurt Child to be able to be

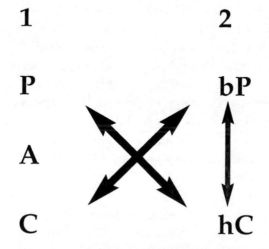

*Figure 4 demonstrates how each party can misperceive the other's emotional state, seeing a Bad Parent instead of the Hurt Child.*

assertive. Assertiveness, the middle of the anger spectrum, is usually more in the domain of the Adult or Good Parent.

Old injuries, current injuries, conflicting needs, transference, Hurt Child ego states, and stylistic differences in communication, as well as the inherent problems of simply hearing and understanding what your partner is saying all add up to making conflict in relationships inevitable. These very conflicts, while they are challenging, are also opportunities for greater closeness and emotional intimacy as we learn to honor each other's difficult feelings and appreciate how they do that for us.

Max and Suzie found a way out of their difficulties. Once Suzie and Max had both calmed down, Max apologized. He admitted to Suzie that he had forgotten their plan and told her that he was truly sorry for doing that. He asked her not to leave and to try to make the best of their time together on that weekend. He asked to reschedule a special weekend with her. He told her that she meant the world to him.

When Suzie realized that he was really sorry, she apologized for having reacted so harshly. She explained that she was simply disappointed about not having him all to herself for the weekend. She agreed to reschedule their special weekend plans. She also said she understood how he had been put in a difficult position with his subcontractor.

Once they had apologized to each other, they began to plan how they could make the time that was left to them more enjoyable. Suzie made plans to spend Saturday afternoon with a friend to exercise and shop while Max supervised the pouring of the foundation. Max made reservations for a special dinner at one of their favorite restaurants. After they had resolved their hurt feelings, they felt even closer than they had before the blow up as a result of appreciating how they had hung in there with each other.

## Stop, Drop, and Roll with Miscommunication Conflicts

Relationship conflicts are inevitable because no one can ever meet all of another person's needs. In my experience with marital and relationship counseling, eighty to ninety-five percent of all relationship conflicts have to do with miscommunication. What this means is that, when you get to the bottom of what was going on, there was no real conflict. It was only that someone got his or her feelings hurt. This is not surprising in light of the concept of transference distortions. It's actually more surprising that people are able to successfully resolve their conflicts at all.

While I already mentioned the Stop, Drop, and Roll model in the context of making dysfunctional anger functional, here I'd like to show how the same steps can be used to resolve miscommunication conflicts. This technique for conflict resolution has come from my years of helping people who are alienated from each other and who have very low levels of trust. It is prescribed and structured so that there are specific ways to proceed in resolving conflict and rebuilding trust, so that the couple might find compassion for each other in their times of injury and use their anger to reconnect emotionally. Each conflict begins with injury, and the angry energy it generates can be used to intervene in an escalation of anger and to build greater trust.

The first step, Stop, is for either party to realize that they are on fire and that there is a conflict taking place. They need to realize that they are both in a Hurt Child ego state and to Stop and take a time out. When at least one of the parties realizes this, they need to ask for the time out, and the partner who's asked needs to honor the request.

If you go back to Max and Suzie's example, things didn't start to improve until they had both settled down. If they were using Stop, Drop, and Roll, the Stop step would mean that either one of them would notice that the argument was escalating. Then they could ask for a time-limited time out. A half an hour might give them the time to reconsider what was happening and limited the extra damage done during escalation.

When both people in the relationship are able to honor a time out, things can calm down. Once everyone is calmed down sufficiently, they can begin to invite each other to join in the Drop step, the step in which the couple will begin to analyze what just happened.

When Max and Suzie got back together to talk, they had both calmed down. Max realized during their time out that he had blown it by forgetting their weekend plans. He also realized that he was feeling defensive. Instead of just apologizing, when he told Suzie about his error he presented all of the reasons why he had to do it. He had never recognized and validated her sense of injury.

During the time out, Suzie realized that she was acting out her Hurt Child anger by scheduling to leave that weekend. She was paying him back, punishing him so that he could feel the same kind of pain that she had felt. She also realized that her anger was cold and passive-aggressive: "You can't make me stay here." She had also gotten aggressive when he confronted her during the escalation.

Now in their Adult ego states, the cognitive task is for the couple to begin to determine whose feelings were hurt first in *this particular conflict*. Don't go back to the beginning of time, which can be very confusing and counter-productive. The process is *not* about finding out whose feelings were hurt at the beginning of the relationship! Keep focused on this conflict. For example, Suzie and Max could have decided that Suzie's feelings got hurt first when Max told her about the conflict. Or they could have decided that Max's feelings were hurt when he realized his error.

Frequently the process by which the couple sorts out whose feelings got hurt first is not as simple or obvious as one might think. Usually, both partners have gotten hurt and believe that their feelings were hurt first. It is normal for the transference dynamics of each partner to have been involved both in the miscommunication and the subsequent conflict.

For example, Max had old injuries about being listened to by his parents. He also had some macho feelings about having to be right. Suzie had abandonment issues from her family that made her jumpy about making commitments. That was part of why she became a stewardess in the first place. She liked to be constantly on the go.

Frequently, when a couple sorts through an injury in my office, it isn't unusual for them to agree about whose feelings got hurt first, while I see it differently. *But it isn't important to be right in your appraisal of whose feelings got hurt first, only that you find an agreement.* If you're focused more on getting it right than in finding agreement, you probably are not in your Adult ego state.

If the couple is able to begin to try to solve this challenge while functioning in their Adult ego states, we have a victory: the couple is beginning to work as a team. But if the question is pursued from the Hurt Child ego state, the conversation is likely to go nowhere. Worse, it can even deteriorate. You can tell that this happening if emotions are flaring up again or if someone is becoming defensive. The challenge is not to be "right" about where it started. This is not about finding blame! If that happens, it's time for another time out, followed by restarting the second step.

This conversation, the Drop step in its entirety, is to be done without any blaming. Blame is poisonous to relationships. Blame is a clue that someone is functioning in their Hurt Child ego state, and another time out would need to be taken. We are not concerned with blame, only function.

It is important to keep in mind that miscommunication conflicts are not about right and wrong. We are only concerned with the emotional injuries. We want to address those injuries and heal them, not to determine whether someone has a right to have them. Whatever feelings you and your partner have, whether you like them or not, they are an integral part of who the two of you are. This includes anger as well as all of the other unpleasant feelings that are part of being human.

The emotions have to be accepted, even if you don't like them and don't think that your partner "should" be having those feelings. Communicating disapproval for your partner's emotional experience is bound to continue the process of injury and argument. It is different for you not to like the feelings that your partner has than to tell them that their feelings are not OK. That difference is very difficult and extremely important to hold onto.

Once the couple agrees on the initial injury, they are ready to proceed to the Roll or action step. This is the Good Parent step in which the couple takes turns acting as a Good Parent to the other's Hurt Child. This means apologizing. The person who was hurt first receives the initial apology and then responds in kind.

It is important to note that when we talk about apology in this situation, it doesn't mean taking blame. This is a *guilt-free, blame-free apology!* The kind of apology I'm talking about here is one in which the person who was hurt second says something like: "I can see that you are feeling hurt, and I want you to know that I never intended to hurt you. I am truly sorry that you were hurt, and I don't want you to be hurt, though I now understand why you were hurt."

To complete this part of the interaction, the person who was hurt first needs to accept the apology in an assertive fashion. This means saying directly "I accept your apology" and adding your thanks.

It is also important for the couple to make direct eye contact while giving and receiving apologies. This, too, can be really hard. It has been said that the eyes are the windows to the soul. If the partners are not ready to look each other in the eye, it is usually because one or both of them are still in their Hurt Child ego state. Making and holding direct eye contact helps to ensure that the apologies are directly received and the emotional bond between the couple is reconnected.

By the way, if one partner truly feels non-neurotic guilt—true remorse—about his or her role in the miscommunication, it's important and appropriate to own it. You should always feel free to make that kind of apology.

To complete the resolution of the first level of the conflict, it is then the responsibility of the person who was hurt first to follow up the apology that they received by apologizing in the same manner. Finally, the person who was hurt second needs to accept the apology assertively as well.

While conflicts frequently escalate, with the partners heaping insult on injury, in my experience, couples usually have to complete apologies for only one level of escalation before they are both feeling that the conflict has been resolved. Rarely, they might feel the need to go to the second level. For example, Max forgot their weekend and Suzie got hurt. She then planned to leave for the weekend to retaliate, and Max got hurt. The second level was started when Max told Suzie to go on and not worry about coming back. Suzie then yelled that she knew he didn't care about her being there in the first place.

In reconnecting, Max and Suzie only had to complete apologies to each other for the first level of their fight. If you find that you need to pursue more than one level on a frequent basis, something other than a sincere attempt to reconnect is going on and you probably need the assistance of a good counselor.

## More About Time Outs

The time out is an important and useful tool in miscommunication conflict resolution. Either partner can call a time out during a conflict when they are feeling either emotionally overwhelmed or stuck and need time to regroup. Time out should be called with a definite time limit, whether this is ten or fifteen minutes, a half hour, after a walk around the block, or even, sometimes, the next day.

The difficulty with calling time out is that frequently one partner is more likely to ask for it. This is because we usually pick people, unconsciously, to balance us on various psychological variables. One partner may be more likely to want to balance the checkbook while the other may not. One is usually more intellectual or rational while the other is more emotional. When you think about it, these kinds of differences are usually positive in that a couple finds balance. However, these same divergent strengths that attract us to our partners can also be experienced as injuries since, because our partner is different and balances us, they will not always behave the way we want and expect. This can be a source of injury and conflict.

In terms of time out, frequently the partner who is not calling for time out will feel some level of abandonment. This can be a problem, especially if that person has family of origin issues related to feeling abandoned, which is very common. Having a deadline for the return to engagement reassures the partner being left that they and their feelings will not be abandoned.

It is also important for the partner calling time out not to use it as a weapon. This happens when there is no time scheduled for reengagement and/or the person calling time out does so in an angry and abusive manner. This indicates that partner's difficulty with the opposite of fear of abandonment: *fear of engulfment*. If someone is suffering from that problem, they will tend to always hold a certain distance in the relationship. They will show a fear of dependency and/or closeness.

Both fear of abandonment and fear of engulfment can be ameliorated by individual work in psychotherapy, though that may take some time. A person's basic dynamic likely won't change, but the intensity of the emotional response can be significantly reduced.

Time outs, when they work effectively, help the couple to reach the second step, Drop, where they can begin to problem solve in a same-team, Adult-to-Adult ego state manner. Time outs serve to reduce the level of damage done by dysfunctional anger being thrown back and forth and to mobilize the couple to use the energy of anger functionally so that they may reconnect.

## Real Conflicts in Intimate Relationships

In contrast to Max and Suzie's communication conflict, real conflicts occur in most relationships from time to time. Barry and Beth are in the midst of a real conflict that needs to be resolved. They are a couple in their late twenties and still in the beginnings of their careers.

They have a two-year-old daughter and Beth is pregnant with their second child. Barry has a funky old Porsche and Beth has been driving a Honda. Barry's old sports car is a beloved remnant of his carefree bachelor days and he babies it. It needs a paint job, but it's in great mechanical condition. He doesn't drive it very much now, but when he was single, he used to race it with his Porsche club on weekends. He mostly drives his even more beat-up old Saab around town.

With their second child on the way, Beth wants Barry to sell his Porsche and Saab and drive the Honda, which is reliable and economical. Beth thinks that Barry needs to trade his Porsche and Saab on a new minivan which she can use to ferry the kids around in safety. Barry can't believe that she would even ask him to do this. He agrees in principle that they need something more reliable for their growing family, but he's upset about the idea of his prized sports car being turned into the family minivan. They really disagree about what to do.

A small number of conflicts, about five to fifteen percent, are real conflicts like Barry and Beth's, and can be hard to resolve. Real conflicts occur when there is no miscommunication. We simply want different things, and both choices are not possible. Real conflicts, as opposed to communication conflicts, are generally resolved in one of three ways. The first resolution isn't a real one, though it's the method most frequently used. The second and third ways are the real ways of resolving real conflicts, and they both represent the concept of fairness.

The first conflict resolution method, the unreal one, is ignoring the conflict, putting it away, and pretending it isn't there. Frequently this leads to problems in the long term, though, at times, people can cope with the problem in the short term. For example, if Barry and Beth were to ignore the problem, they might continue on with the same cars and the same dynamic. They might have the same fight over and over again, month after month, and never resolve it. Both of them would become more and more resentful.

Maybe one day Barry would do something about it or maybe one day Beth would tell him to find an apartment. Maybe they'd stay together, quiet and resentful, while their relationship turned into a sour and distant marriage.

The second method is much more realistic—compromise. If one person wants to eat Mexican food for dinner, and the other wants to eat Italian, they might both decide that they could be happy with Chinese. When compromise works, it's fine. If Barry and Beth wanted to compromise, they might agree that Barry could keep his Porsche, but use it as his main car. He could sell the Saab and the Honda, and take out a small loan to buy the new minivan.

When compromise doesn't work, the third alternative is taking turns, the third method of conflict resolution. One person might be willing to accept Italian or Mexican food if the agreement is that their next meal is the one that they originally wanted. Taking turns can build trust because each partner learns that they can count on the other to follow through with agreements. They also learn that they can count on getting their needs met in the relationship most of the time. Barry and Beth could take turns by agreeing that Barry would sell the Porsche and the Saab to buy the minivan, but when the Honda wears out, he could buy himself another second-hand Porsche.

If there is a problem with follow-through in taking turns, however, as in passive-aggressive/hostile dependent relationships, then it has the opposite effect. When people don't follow through on their agreements, it injures the other partner and draws their anger. These kinds of little betrayals erode the trust that relationships are built on. As the trust deteriorates, the couple then launches into a downward spiral of more injury, anger, and distrust. If Barry and Beth had a passive-aggressive/hostile-dependent relationship, Barry might agree to Beth's suggestion that he sell his Porsche and Saab to buy the minivan. Then he would not do it. Then, every time Beth would ask him when he was going to sell it, he'd say "Soon." Eventually, Beth would become furious.

## Passive-Aggressive/Hostile-Dependent Relationships

If Barry continued to act in this passive-aggressive manner, it would represent the cold side of the spectrum of anger. The passive-aggressive/hostile-dependent relationship exists when one of the parties suffers from a tendency to behave like Barry by making agreements and then refusing to follow through. This behavior is one of the most powerful and destructive interpersonal behaviors. Another example of passive-aggressive behavior would be if I said that I'd meet you at noon for lunch at a certain restaurant and then I showed up a half an hour late with no explanation or apology, you would be likely to feel the injury and anger that my passive-aggressive behavior anger has caused.

When someone plays the passive-aggressive game of "You can't make me" in a relationship, it is extremely destructive, since relationships are based on agreements. This is very angry behavior, but instead of looking angry in the traditional sense of the word it draws the anger of the hostile-dependent partner toward the passive-aggressive partner.

The hostile-dependent partner usually expresses the anger for both players, and there is usually a lot of anger. It can escalate, too. The reality is that the total anger expressed in a passive-aggressive/hostile-dependent interaction is really comprised of the anger of both partners—current, here-and-now anger as well as their "old business" anger. (See Figure 5.)

Barry and Beth had a real conflict related to selling Barry's sports car for the safety of the family. While Barry really didn't want to sell his prized possession, he saw the logic of it. However, Barry had a tendency to be passive-aggressive in the relationship. For Barry, this style was one that was developed early in his childhood. Barry's father and mother were both alcoholics and their home was full of constant chaos and abuse. His parents would get into violent drunken fights. His father was surly all the time, even when he was sober. Barry's mother would swat him and his three younger sisters when they were little. When they were older she would threaten

# Dynamics of Anger

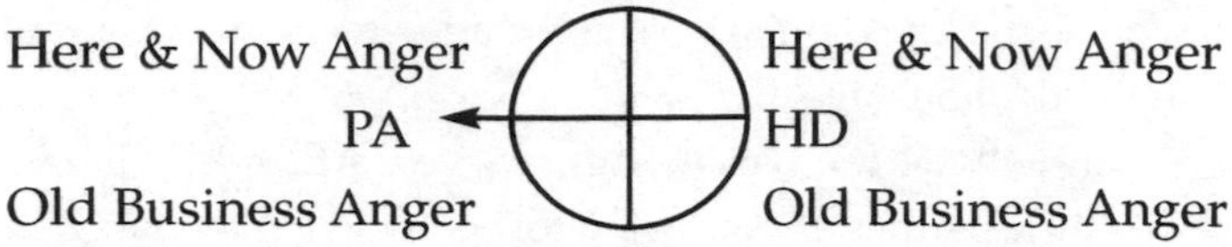

Here & Now Anger          Here & Now Anger
PA                        HD
Old Business Anger        Old Business Anger

*Figure 5: The dynamics of anger in the passive-aggressive/hostile-dependent relationship*

Barry with "Wait 'til your father comes home!"

Barry learned early on not to count on his parents for love and support. He also learned to be terrified of conflict. This played out in his relationship with Beth in that he would agree to almost anything Beth asked him to do. Since she was staying home to take care of their young daughter, Beth depended on Barry a lot. So, when Beth suggested that Barry part with his Porsche, he agreed. It made sense to sell it. They did need a safe, reliable family car.

But Barry really didn't want to sell it. He traded in the Saab right away for an Astrovan, but he put off selling the Porsche. His reasoning was that he could get more money for the Porsche if he sold it himself—but then he procrastinated on advertising it in the paper.

Beth was concerned because they needed the money to finance a lower payment on the Astrovan and the Porsche was sitting in the driveway. Barry came up with excuses. The Porsche needed some work before he could sell it. It needed to be painted. Each time Beth asked, Barry had another excuse.

After three months of not having the Porsche advertised for sale, Beth blew up at Barry one night. She yelled at him and accused him of never intending to sell it. Barry, of course, became defensive and told her he was working on it. He told her to be patient. When this didn't calm Beth, Barry retreated and was cold and distant with her for several days. While he wasn't aware of it, he was punishing her.

There are all kinds of psychological dynamics to this type of relationship. The hostile-dependent partner gets to be justified in

his or her anger, and to be right. Beth was clearly "right," and felt secure in her anger at Barry. The passive-aggressive partner gets to do what he or she likes, regardless of the agreements and commitments in the relationship.

Eventually, if the passive-aggressive partner isn't able to realize that their partner doesn't want to, and won't, play the game, the hostile-dependent partner leaves the relationship. The exception to this would be when the transference on the part of the hostile-dependent partner is so strong that she or he can never let go of trying to get the passive-aggressive partner to change. This was clearly the case for Beth, who grew up in a family where her father, too, was an alcoholic. Her father became extremely angry when drunk, and dangerous as well.

Beth learned in her family that her mother's way of dealing with her father didn't work. Beth's mother was terrified and intimidated by her husband and would use the five children to shield herself from her husband when he was out of control. Beth could see that this didn't work and would confront her father when he was sober. Her father would be apologetic when he was sober, but it would only be a matter of time until the cycle started over again.

This dynamic from Beth's childhood left her stuck trying to get Barry to see the error of his ways. While she didn't feel good to be in conflict so often with Barry, she was committed to getting him to change. In fact, Barry and Beth's transference dynamics bound them closely together. She would try to convince him to change and feel justified about being angry. He would feel equally justified in resenting her explosions and then withdraw, since, based on his volatile childhood, he was committed to not having any emotional outbursts in his marriage.

The passive-aggressive partner usually is operating out of a combination of both fear and anger. Fear gets him to agree to things that he really doesn't want to agree to. The rage that passive-aggressive behavior can elicit only serves to confirm that he needs to continue to be fearful, and the passive-aggressive partner doesn't

recognize the angry aspects of what he is doing.

When the hostile-dependent partner is truly done with trying to make the passive-aggressive partner change, either she leaves the relationship or the passive-aggressive partner realizes that no one is trying to "make" him do anything. When the hostile-dependent partner stops playing the game, the passive-aggressive partner then has to decide what he wants to do, rather than only respond to the feeling of being compelled.

Passive-aggressive/hostile-dependent dynamics can complicate and confound a couple trying to use Stop, Drop, and Roll to resolve either real conflicts, like the one Barry and Beth were having, or miscommunication conflicts such as Max and Suzie's. These characteristic personality styles, which are frequently enmeshed with the transference dynamics of intense childhood injury and trauma, tend to keep people in their Hurt Child ego states when they become injured, making it hard to recover. If you can't recover, it's hard to Drop and get grounded and move into an Adult ego state. If you can't understand what's going on, it's hard to Roll into a caring Parental behavior.

Passive-aggressive partners can realize that they are behaving that way if they usually retreat in their relationship and find that their partners frequently get hurt and angry. Those who are passive-aggressive tend to withdraw and refuse to communicate. They harbor resentments and their partners keep pointing out their failure to follow through on agreements. Hostile-dependent partners know they're in a passive-aggressive/hostile-dependent relationship if they're always getting angry at their partner for breaking agreements and denying that there were agreements. They feel justified in venting their anger.

Usually, it is the hostile-dependent partner who identifies the dynamic of passive-aggression in the relationship, though it can take a while. When she becomes fed up with being angry and frustrated all the time, she will most likely talk with friends, find a self-help book, or ask to go into counseling.

That was the case with Beth and Barry. They didn't go into counseling over the Porsche. They didn't get to that point for another year. However, Beth approached Barry, finally, without any hostility. She simply told him that they had a problem and that she needed his help in resolving it. She told him that he obviously didn't want to sell his Porsche and that she understood his attachment. She presented it without emotion and asked what he thought was a good solution.

When Barry realized that Beth wasn't going to make him sell his Porsche, he had to decide if he wanted to keep it and struggle to pay more on the loan for their minivan, or sell it and drive the Honda. He decided to keep his Porsche and sell the Honda to get a lower minivan payment. He thought it would cost more in the future for him to buy another Porsche, and realized he would resent Beth if he sold it. Even though Beth would have preferred he sell the Porsche, she was relieved to have the struggle resolved.

## A Few Final Thoughts About Intimacy

While being intimate is the hardest thing to do in life, it is also the most rewarding. Whether you listen to Woody Allen tell you that "You still need the eggs" or the Beatles sing "Love is all you need," intimacy seems to be a truly universal need. And, while "all you need is love," the love is the easy part. Dealing with people is much more challenging than merely loving them. And the hardest part of dealing with people is dealing with conflict, anger, and other difficult emotions.

You can find more love, and make it more fulfilling, if you're willing to use the anger that comes from injury in relationships to do the work for which it is meant—fixing the injuries to both partners. Use the Stop, Drop, and Roll method for unbending the anger to become emotionally closer and more fulfilled with each other. It won't be easy, but it is rewarding to stay focused and develop the process with each other over time. While it can happen, it's very unusual for a couple to not be able to work out their differences if they stay committed to doing the hard work of dealing with conflict and their difficult emotions.

Beware of cold, passive-aggressive anger. It can be just as dysfunctional in relationships as hot, aggressive anger, and just as destructive. Beth and Barry suffered from the dynamics of a passive-aggressive/hostile-dependent relationship. It was present for Max and Suzie as well. Max's "forgetting" represented some unconscious pain and anger on his part. He had his own conflict with his need to take care of his business and his need to be with Suzie.

Another very simple piece of advice that I give to clients when they begin relationship counseling is to be nice to each other. It seems easy, when trust has been seriously injured, to stay in your Hurt Child with your partner, nurture your resentments instead of your relationship, and keep throwing barbs at each other. But this is terribly painful and harmful to both of you. It is challenging, but much more rewarding, to be nice to each other and to work to give each other the benefit of the doubt.

Above all, remember that blame is poison. It is the most dysfunctional use of anger you can have in an intimate relationship. A simple way to remember this is to notice that, if you are pointing your finger at someone, there are always three fingers pointing back at you. In relationships, pointing the finger is an assault with a dangerous weapon. When you want to blame your partner, if you can be aware of that feeling, you would be best served to Stop, Drop, and Roll into looking at how you can change your dysfunctional anger into behaviors that will bring you the love you want.

If you truly want to be able to find the compassion and caring you seek, it's very important to make sure that you are giving it. It is always easier to see your partner's vulnerabilities and difficulties than it is to see your own. If you do believe that your partner loves you, then giving to your partner is one of the most helpful things you can do.

CHAPTER 8

# How Do You Heal the Hole in Your Heart?

## *"All You Need Is Love!"*

JOHN LENNON AND PAUL MCCARTNEY SANG "ALL YOU
need is love." And I agree that the hole in your heart can only be
filled with love. But how does one do that?

It's hard to heal the hole in your heart, the original injuries
that generated so much pain, sadness, and fear and caused us to
learn to use our anger in dysfunctional ways. It takes tremendous
courage and dedication. I'm constantly in awe of my clients who
against all odds work to heal, prevail, and flourish. While there are
no definitive road maps to healing, there is a gyroscope, a sense of
direction that you can find inside of yourself. Most of us need help
with that process, and while others in your life may help, it is the
specific domain of a good psychotherapist.

How do we undo the lack of love, or worse, the actual abuse
that happened during childhood? How do we learn to love, to trust,
and to emotionally connect with others? How do we connect with
our own anger and that of those we love without having it become
dysfunctional? How do we maintain our own power without getting lost in it?

The simple answer is that the Internalized Parent, the Bad
Parent of your childhood, needs to be confronted and changed into
a Good Parent. That Internalized Parent voice needs to be one that
is supportive, nurturing, and consistently coming to you with loving energy.

But how can we make that happen?

The first half of the battle is to make the commitment that

you're willing to do whatever it takes to recover from your injuries. Many of us don't like the vulnerability of accepting that we have an injury, and we all have some resistance to even admitting we might need help. Some of us have been so conditioned to avoid our feelings that we can't even see that the injury is there. Healing, and especially psychotherapy, can be experienced as the insult to the injury. It's bad enough to be injured in the first place, and to have to spend time, money, and energy to recover is truly unfair. However, we pursue therapy because of our intrinsic need to heal.

Not everyone's injuries are severe enough to require therapy, and most people find that they can live successfully without a full healing. However, even with parents who love you, their inherited dysfunction can damage your self-esteem and your ability to relate well to others. Both of these areas can cause us to lose both our effectiveness and our enjoyment of life.

So, again, what do we do with the emotional injuries? We all get them, of course, at different levels of intensity, and we all have different natural, genetic abilities to absorb injury. What's a slight injury to someone may be a significant trauma to another. If injury isn't experienced in the family, it usually can be found with our peers as we struggle to grow up in a competitive and frequently unsupportive world.

This chapter is meant to describe the basic dynamics that are involved in a full healing process. To understand this process you have to start by looking at the way that the hole in your heart was first created. Let's revisit the figure from Chapter Three in which I describe the internal relationships of the Bad Parent, "Good" Kid, and "Bad" Kid (see diagram below). These dynamics take place within each of us. The arrows represent the communication among these internal parts of us, with intersected or broken lines showing problems.

To review, the definition of a Bad Parent is anyone who parents out of his or her Hurt Child ego state. The central message of a Bad Parent is, in effect, saying to their child: "I'm not here to take care of you; you are here to take care of me." This is a reversal of

## Dynamics of Dysfunction

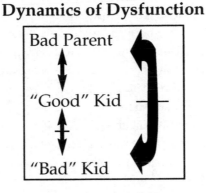

*Figure 1*

roles and is a result of the Bad Parent's emotional neediness. This neediness comes from the Bad Parent suffering some emotional injury that overwhelms their Adult and Parent ego states while they are parenting.

Again, remember that there are no perfect parents and that every parent behaves this way at times. This isn't meant to be an indictment of parents, merely an attempt to understand and heal from the dynamics of injury.

The Bad Parent's interaction with the child causes the child to experience a split into a "Good" Kid and a "Bad" Kid. The child's survival instinct causes the "Good" Kid to respond positively to the Bad Parent's dysfunctional and injurious request. Since the Bad Parent is a giant with the power of life and death over the child, the "Good" Kid will do whatever it takes to survive. The "Good" Kid is the caretaker/victim, willing to attend to others, even at their own expense.

A common example is when a parent is parenting while depressed or irritable. If a parent is hungry or tired, they may deliver a smaller version of the Bad Parent message than an alcoholic parent. If a parent is going through a divorce, it is likely that there will be times when they are too upset and injured themselves to be able to be a Good Parent to their child. The child then can be coerced into the caretaking role of the "Good" Kid.

Meanwhile, another part of the child—the "Bad" Kid—is hurt, sad, scared, and angry. The "Bad" Kid is more associated with Freud's concept of the Id, the primitive emotional being. The "Bad" Kid really doesn't care about what transpires between the "Good" Kid and the Bad Parent. The "Bad" Kid either acts out her anger directly, by confronting the Bad Parent, or is subdued by the "Good" Kid. When the "Bad" Kid is subjugated, her anger has to go somewhere dysfunctional since it isn't being used directly to fix what is hurting her.

Healing cannot take place while the "Good" Kid is aligned with the Bad Parent and alienated from the "Bad" Kid. As long as the split between the "Bad" Kid and "Good" Kid is unresolved, the anger in the system will continue to flow into some form of emotional dysfunction. This is what I mean by "bent" anger. The anger for the Bad Parent is misdirected. It may go into exaggerating fears into anxiety or into depression. It may go into explosive anger, addictive behaviors, or relationship problems. Whatever form it takes, this dysfunctional anger will continue to cause problems in some way.

Much has been written about "healing the inner child." I believe that in healing the split between the "Bad" Kid and "Good" Kid, you have healed the inner child, but that this is only the first part of the healing process. I like to call this first piece *Empowering the Inner Child*, since healing the split leads clients to find or rediscover their ability to use their anger and power more effectively. When the "Good" Kid and "Bad" Kid are working together, anger is no longer bent into a loop that causes it to work against your self, causing dysfunction.

The most important use of the anger of the empowered inner child in the healing process is to force the Internalized Parent figure to deal with the injuries that it has caused while functioning as a Bad Parent. This is not a simple process. It involves having the

Bad Parent realize the errors that they have made, apologize, and stop behaving this way.

Let's revisit George, who had that famous panic attack in San Francisco on his honeymoon. To get his anxiety under control, George worked with his therapist, Alan, once he was back in Chicago. At the beginning of treatment, they focused mostly on short-term work using Stop, Drop, and Roll and George took the medications provided by his psychiatrist.

As his therapy with Alan progressed, George realized that he had spent most of his life as a "Good" Kid who took care of his mother, Marilyn. George also realized that he had been afraid of abandonment, and that this was related to the distancing he experienced with his father, William. Once George's panic and anxiety were under control he decided that he wanted to work through those injuries to make sure he wouldn't fall back into anxiety.

George had already been working on assertiveness and on unbending his anger using the Stop, Drop, and Roll system to intervene in his anxiety. But that same process was also changing the balance between his "Good" and "Bad" Kid positions. Nonetheless, as he began to work to confront his Internal Mother and Father during role-playing in therapy, he would often find his anger blocked by his "Good" Kid. When that would occur, George would have to refocus the anger toward confronting his "Good" Kid to get him to stop blocking his "Bad" Kid from delivering the anger where it belonged: his Internal Mother and Internal Father.

This felt dangerous. His "Good" Kid would be stuck feeling that he was protecting the "Bad" Kid from confronting the Internal Parents in order to survive. His "Bad" Kid was angry about the "Good" Kid's protection of the Bad Parent. His "Good" Kid and "Bad" Kid struggled with each other. George's "Good" Kid had spent so many years protecting those parents from his "Bad" Kid's anger that it was habitual and comfortable. Gradually, as George's "Bad" Kid argued and bargained with his "Good" Kid, their relationship improved to the point that George could begin to confront his

Internalized Parents as an empowered inner child. His "Good" and "Bad" Kids could work together to use his anger appropriately.

This next stage of George's treatment also had to develop gradually. Initially, both his Bad Mom and Bad Dad resisted the confrontation. However, over time, George's "Good" Kid continued to stay out of his "Bad" Kid's way. His "Bad" Kid continued to confront his Internal Bad Parents and learned to fight through their defenses. Eventually, George's "Bad" Kid was able to convince first his Internal Mother and then his Internal Father to admit to the mistakes they had made in parenting him. In fact, his Internal Parents sincerely apologized and promised to make it up to him by supporting him in the future.

Once this transition is accomplished, the Bad Parent becomes a Good Parent—internally, at least. This is what full healing is truly all about. I call the whole process *Empowering the Inner Child to Heal the Internalized Parent.*

It's important to understand the difference between the Internal Parent and the External Parent. The External Parent is the one that is either walking around as an independent human being or is dead. The Internal Parent is what we have absorbed of our parents' personalities from how they treated us while we were growing up. You can find the Internal Parent in the act of role-playing, when you act out the Bad Parent's role in a self-dialogue. This type of work is referred to as Gestalt therapy. Since the real human parent isn't in the room, the only parent you could be dealing with is the Internalized Parent.

## Julia's Story

To clarify these concepts, let's look at the case of Julia. Julia, the older of two children, grew up with a mother who was severely narcissistic, anxious, and depressed. Her father had died when Julia was quite young. Julia's mother, Maureen, was never all that strong emotionally. When her husband, Gary, died of a heart attack, Maureen fell apart.

Gary had supported Maureen and the kids in an upper-middle class lifestyle, and Maureen didn't work outside of the home. She tended to the kids and had time to exercise and play tennis at her club. She was involved with a group of other young mothers whose main focus was their social life. When Gary died, although there was a significant life insurance policy, Maureen was overwhelmed. She was often depressed and anxious, and unknowingly asked Julia not to need much attention or caring from her. Maureen conveyed these messages both verbally and nonverbally, and Julia began to take care of her mother's emotional and physical needs at an early age.

Julia became caretaker to her younger brother, Sam, as well as to her mother. Her "Good" Kid was there for her mother and for her brother. Julia's "Bad" Kid was suppressed, and she wasn't even aware of the pain and anger that this caused her. Not only had she lost her father, she had lost her childhood, too.

When Julia was in her late twenties, she found her way into therapy because she suffered from anxiety and all her relationships seemed to fail. The relationships seemed to go along fine until she began expressing her emotional needs. When she asked for her needs to be met, she was usually dumped very quickly.

As Julia began to sort through this information with her therapist, she discovered that she had a pattern of unconsciously choosing emotionally distant and narcissistic men. She had done what was familiar to her. She had learned that if you wanted to be loved, you needed to take care of others, and she did that very well. Partly because of the loss of her father, she unconsciously needed to reenact that abandonment. Partly due to her mother's self-involvement, she needed, again unconsciously, to have a somewhat narcissistic partner so that she could try to change him. If she could change her partner and get him to see that she was worth the effort of changing, it would correct her experience of growing up emotionally abandoned.

Her mother and father were not there with her when she was choosing partners who shared these difficult psychological traits. However, the Internal Parents are always with us, and those voices were part of Julia's unconscious choices. "Don't take care of you, take care of me," was the refrain from her Internal Mother. Her Internal Father chimed in with "You can't count on me to be there for you." Julia needed, at the very least, to be aware of the voices and change her choices for partnership. Ideally, she needed to change the Internal Parent voices from Bad Parent voices to Good Parent voices so that she wouldn't continue to be negatively attracted to men who duplicated these Internal Bad Parent messages. This kind of attraction to negative messages in relationships is another form of transference and what Harville Hendrix talks about in his "Imago" therapy.

While the concept of the Internal Parent may seem simple on paper, frequently clients initially struggle with differentiating between the Internal Parent and the External Parent. When the client realizes that his or her difficulties are a function of the parent that has been internalized, the healing work can begin.

If his or her parent is still alive, the client may be intimidated by the idea of losing that real-life parent through the process of therapy. This can occasionally happen. If it does, it is usually a function of the client gaining personal strength though psychotherapy and the living parent's inability to deal with the boundaries that their child is now setting. Usually, however, this alienation usually lasts only briefly while the internal changes take place within the client. To some extent, it depends on the level of damage or pathology in the parent.

A client who is truly healed is able to be more effective in setting boundaries with her or his parents in real life. This happens because the client no longer *needs* the approval of that parent. The client may still want that approval, but there is no longer a sense of desperation to get it. Of course there are parents who continue to be truly toxic—actively psychologically and emotionally destructive—to their children, and in that case the client may have to close that relationship. In addition, there are parents who are so narcissistic that they cannot tolerate the boundaries that their children set, and passive-aggressively retreat and close the relationship from the parental side.

This rejection by one's parents, if it happens, can be very painful for clients. It is a risk of treatment. In the course of uncovering unresolved hurts and angers with the Internal Parents, it may become very difficult for clients not to confront their parents in real life. I try to encourage clients to be very thoughtful about these risks and if, how, and when to begin to deal with any confrontation with their parents in real life.

### Transitioning to Healing

Whether we are looking at George's experience in therapy, Julia's, or yours, in long-term treatment the dynamics of healing are the same. Internal changes need to happen in how the client functions emotionally. Anger related to childhood injuries needs to be mobilized to become functional and change the relational dynamics between the "Good" Kid, the "Bad" Kid, and the Internalized Bad Parent.

The diagram below shows the transition in these relationships from being damaged to being healed.

In this diagram, in the unhealed individual we see that there are three important and internal dyadic relationships (relationships

## Dynamics of Healing

**Damaged Individual**          **Healed Individual**

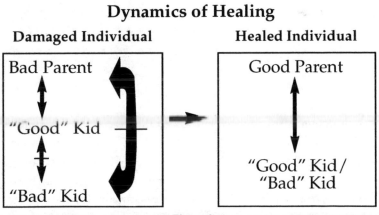

*Figure 6*

**THE HEALING POWER OF ANGER**

between two entities). Therefore, three transitions need to take place within an individual in their healing process. Each transition relates to one of these internal relationships. The relationship between the Bad Parent and the "Good" Kid needs to change. Also, the relationship between the "Good" Kid and the "Bad" Kid needs to change. Finally, the relationship between the Bad Parent and "Bad" Kid needs to change as well.

Usually there is a mix in an individual's process of working on these transitions. A client may need to move back and forth between working on the "Good" Kid/"Bad" Kid dyad and experimenting with a confrontation between the "Bad" Kid and the Bad Parent. However, frequently the initial focus is on the relationship between the "Good" Kid and "Bad" Kid. Additionally, the last dyad to change usually is the Bad Parent and the "Bad" Kid. Usually, the client doesn't need to work directly on the relationship between the Bad Parent and the "Good" Kid, even though that relationship needs to change as well. This dyad usually changes as a result of the confrontations between the "Good" Kid and "Bad" Kid. What happens is that the "Good" Kid does less caretaking of the Bad Parent over time and sets more boundaries.

The first thing that needs to happen is that the "Good" Kid and "Bad" Kid must be reunited. This relationship transition is what I believe therapists mean when they talk about healing the inner child. I like to think of this as *Empowering the Inner Child*. There are no divisions within us as infants. This split is developed in response to the quintessential Bad Parent message: "I'm not here to take care of you; you need to take care of me." The "Good" Kid and "Bad" Kid need to realize that they are on the same side.

In family therapy, we talk about the process of differentiation from the family of origin. What this means is that a person begins to define himself in the world on his own terms, instead of how the family that he grew up in might define him. The child is no longer content to merely play out the script about his or her identity that the parents have created. In my system of thinking about this process, differentiation from the family of origin means a change in the dyad of Bad Parent and "Good" Kid. This bond is broken, which is not easy, due to the "Good" Kid's anxiety involved in the need to please the Bad Parent in order to survive.

Most of us start out having our "Good" Kid aligned with our Bad Parent. Our "Bad" Kid is the frustrated outsider. In this process of differentiation, we also need to develop a new relationship between the "Good" Kid and "Bad" Kid. Many times, when clients role-play these different parts of themselves, it is almost like marriage counseling, as the "Good" Kid and "Bad" Kid express feelings, bargain, and form a more functional relationship. Frequently, the dialogue between these internal parts of our selves begins the process of growth.

In this first stage of healing, there are two basic transitions that need to take place within the psyche. These transitions take place simultaneously, so, in mentioning them here, the order is not important. One transition, again, is for the alliance of Bad Parent and "Good" Kid to be broken (differentiation from the family of origin). The other transition is for the alliance between the "Good" Kid and "Bad" Kid to be strengthened (empowering the inner child). Eventually, this will lead to the creation of an intact alliance between the "Good" Kid and "Bad" Kid, with the establishment of a better boundary between Bad Parent and "Good" Kid.

Most of the clients who make it into therapy are functioning mainly in the "Good" Kid mode, and the therapist needs to ally with the isolated and downtrodden "Bad" Kid. The therapist does this by validating the feelings of the client, whether the client is aware of these feelings or not. This can be tricky, because clients who are truly stuck in the "Good" Kid mode are likely to resist accepting the feelings coming from either their own "Bad" Kid or the therapist.

Succeeding in the face of this kind of challenge requires that the therapist use all of her or his intuition and creativity. If the client-therapist relationship is strong enough and the therapist can reach the client with an explanation of the resistance, the therapist's support of the "Bad" Kid will help the transition to a healthy

"Good" Kid/"Bad" Kid alliance by lending support to the client's emotional being. "Bad" Kids are usually ganged up on by both the "Good" Kid and the Bad Parent. Additionally, the Bad Parent may have many other allies in authority, such as a church, teachers or coaches, etc. The support of the therapist for the "Bad" Kid helps to even the balance in the conflict.

Dealing with a client who has chosen a more "Bad" Kid stance in life can be even trickier. The therapist still needs to align with the "Bad" Kid. However, the therapist also needs to work to strengthen the "Good" Kid. Frequently people who have maintained a life role of "Bad" Kid have messed up their lives pretty significantly by acting out their anger with drugs, alcohol, or even criminal behavior. The "Bad" Kid sees the therapist as someone who, while aligned with his or her emotional being, is also able to function successfully in the world. The "Bad" Kid client wants to learn how to be integrated and more successful in the world, but he or she also may be fearful that the therapist will turn out to be just another Bad Parent authority figure that will betray him or her. There can be all kinds of testing in the context of the therapy relationship, but this dynamic can be present for all therapy relationships.

Once the therapist is connected to the "Bad" Kid, the two of them can begin to work to break the alliance of Bad Parent/"Good" Kid. *The "Bad" Kid's anger is the energy which fuels the whole healing process,* beginning with the confrontation between "Good" Kid and "Bad" Kid. The "Bad" Kid's anger is needed to help the "Good" Kid break away from the Bad Parent, which the "Good" Kid is afraid to do. The "Good" Kid may try to punish the "Bad" Kid and sabotage this process by diverting the anger into "Good" Kid Backlash. "Good" Kid Backlash can be experienced as the two steps back clients often make when they have begun to be more assertive and connected to their "Bad" Kid.

Frequently, when the "Good" Kid and "Bad" Kid begin to interact, there is a great deal of resentment and fear. Just like many other problematic relationships, when the two parts begin to work with each other, it can start out pretty rocky. There can be lots of conflict. Anger can flow in both directions. Generally, over time, however, they begin to deal with each other more successfully. Frequently, the relationship evolves as the "Good" Kid and "Bad" Kid begin to realize how much they need and depend on each other. At this point, there usually is the beginning of a bargaining process. Eventually they go beyond conflict resolution toward trust and a sense of integration, where there is less polarization. This, then, is the healing or empowering of the inner child.

## Healing the Internalized Bad Parent

As "Good" Kid and "Bad" Kid move toward resolution, they can begin to work as a team on the second transition. This change is the conversion of the Internal Bad Parent into a Good Parent and truly healing the hole in one's heart. Again, while there are the basic dynamics for this process, there are no clear road maps. Each person involved in healing has a somewhat different path toward healing the Internalized Bad Parent.

This doesn't necessarily mean a break in the relationship with one's actual parents, but it certainly can happen when one or more of the real-life (external) parents are toxic to the client. Even if the External Parent isn't completely toxic, the client may need a period of separation from the parent's influence to solidify his therapeutic changes. While this may be painful, if it is handled well, it usually isn't incredibly disruptive.

As the "Good" Kid and "Bad" Kid begin to work together effectively, the "Good" Kid either ceases or at least significantly decreases its interference in the second part of the healing process: confronting the Internalized Bad Parent. I like to characterize this confrontation by the phrase the "Bad" Kid brings to the Bad Parent: "You owe me a Good Parent, and I'm here to collect ... and I'm not taking 'no' for an answer!"

This can be a difficult emotional process. The Internal Bad Parent usually doesn't just give up after the first confrontation.

although sometimes clients may wish or hope for that. It usually requires the "Bad" Kid's anger to be delivered to the Internal Bad Parent. I've seen clients do a role-play where the Bad Parent instantaneously relents and apologizes in an unrealistic manner. Unfortunately, this kind of superficial process usually doesn't heal the injuries. For the transformation to take place, the Bad Parent needs to change internally in a way that causes the client to feel like a real transition has taken place in the Internalized Parent. This may take months or years of ongoing role-playing confrontations.

It's not unusual for the Bad Parent to continue to try all of its old tricks in a series of confrontations. It may try to lure the "Good" Kid back into alliance with every manipulative trick in the book. The Bad Parent may plead ignorance, elicit guilt (a classic), beg, threaten to withdraw love and approval, threaten abandonment, or play "poor me." The Bad Parent may explain all the reasons why the client with a newly integrated "Good" Kid and "Bad" Kid "should" take care of the Bad Parent's needs and abandon his or her own needs once again. This is a repetition of the essence of Bad Parenting, when the parent asks the child to take care of the parent's emotional needs instead of the parent attending to the needs of the child.

Due to the new alliance of the "Good" Kid and the "Bad" Kid, the client can begin to use his or her emotions more effectively. Clients can now use their anger to force their Internalized Bad Parent to deal with the injuries that they have caused their child. One of the nice things about role-playing with an Internalized Bad Parent is that they cannot use the passive-aggressive retreat that External Parents can use. Parents in real life can refuse to deal with a client. The Internalized Parent can't use that retreat unless the client allows that behavior, and a good therapist will not let a client make that mistake.

Making the Bad Parent experience the pain and sadness that he or she has caused their child seems to make a difference. The power of the client's emotions can break through their Bad Parent's narcissism and elicit a Good Parent. The Bad Parent is able to make the corrective changes necessary to leave his or her own Hurt Child ego state and assume the appropriate Good Parent ego state for the benefit of his or her actual child, the client.

Their are many clients, however, whose Internal Parent is so severely damaged that they can not even imagine their Internal Parent as being able to heal and make the transition into a Good Parent. The narcissism that they experienced in their parent or parents in their childhood makes the idea seem like nothing more than wishful thinking.

These clients must work to replace their Internal Parent with images of other people who have played the Good Parent role. This may include many different caretakers: other siblings, grandparents, aunts, uncles, maids, teachers, parents of friends, partners, and so on. This synthetic Good Parent may have parts of Good Parents contributed from movies or books as well. Frequently, visualization, hypnosis, and/or eye movement techniques are helpful in this process. Of course, this synthetic Good Parent may include the image of the client's therapist. Good therapists frequently play the role of Good Parent in addition to the many other roles.

My favorite science-fiction author of all time is Orson Scott Card, who writes incredibly thoughtful and provocative character studies of people in extreme and unusual circumstances. In *Songmaster*, he describes a period of time when his hero, the young boy Ansset, is taken by his teacher, Esste, and locked in the High Room of the Songhouse. Ansset is a true genius and has been kidnapped from his loving parents at an early age. He carries those emotional injuries, which interfere in his reaching his potential as a "songbird." Esste keeps Ansset locked in the high room with her, holding him and loving him as he goes through the emotional catharsis that he needs, until his heart is healed.

I've always seen this experience in Card's story as a powerful and beautiful metaphor for therapy. Psychotherapy is a creative process limited only by the creativity and imagination of the client and therapist. It must take place in a safe environment. The therapist must find the way to be present, giving, and caring within the appropriate boundaries, in order to have the client's fears and injuries resolved.

Another metaphor I like is that of the therapist as gardener. The gardener plants the seed, loves and protects the seedling as it becomes a plant, and provides good soil, nutrients, water, and sunshine. As the plant develops, with all of the caring conditions provided, it will find its way to its full growth and flowering. As the therapist provides the wisdom, safety, and nurturing that the client needs, the client finds his way to his recovery and his flowering, and healing the hole in his heart.

In closing this chapter, I'd like to leave you with the love song from *Songmaster*. I find it to be both poignant and powerful. It communicates the very primitive feelings of the young child, full of love in its basic simplicity. It is sung first to Ansset, early in the book by Rruk, a five-year-old girl. Rruk takes the three-year-old Ansset under her wing when he first arrives at the Songhouse, lonely, vulnerable, and desolate after his kidnapping. Rruk sings:

> *"I will never hurt you.*
> *I will always help you.*
> *If you are hungry*
> *I'll give you my food.*
> *If you are frightened*
> *I am your friend.*
> *I love you now*
> *And love does not end."*

# CHAPTER 9

# Doing Whatever It Takes

THROUGHOUT THIS BOOK I HAVE EXPRESSED MY AWE for the courage and conviction of my clients. In spite of injuries that are frequently powerful and occasionally horrific, my clients persevere and find ways to use their anger to fight through anxiety, problems with mood, and addictive behaviors so that they may achieve emotional health and fulfillment. I hope to leave you inspired to take on the healing work you deserve and require, just as my clients do.

In thinking about my clients and their path toward healing, I recall the movie *Network*. Its most famous line is when one of the main characters gets really angry and opens a window and yells, "I'm mad as hell and I'm not going to take it anymore!" This is the attitude you want to have when working to defeat the emotional problems in your life. Getting over the hump in therapy or creating more personal growth is making the commitment to yourself that you are going to do whatever it takes to make your life more fulfilling.

Anger is the energy that powers that commitment. The injuries you have experienced, along with dysfunctional uses of the anger that was meant for attending to the injury, has kept you away from the commitment to do what you must do to recover. As you begin to have the energy of anger to use functionally, it will support your commitment to do what it takes for you to heal.

Once you reach this level of commitment, the unfolding of your process becomes much easier. Reaching the commitment to do whatever it takes means that you will have passed most of the resistance to your healing process. You will understand that caring for yourself is an ongoing, daily experience. You'll see where therapy or other healing behaviors fit into your process. Instead of working to realize your anger and hunt for its dysfunction, you'll be in touch with it and use it functionally to attend to your here-and-now injuries. You'll also understand how those injuries resonate with the old injuries, whether you focus on working on the old business or not.

This doesn't mean that you won't have to sort through difficult feelings or that you won't resist it at times. Healing, at whatever level, requires your dedication and persistence, but it will feel more like you're going downhill rather than, like Sisyphus, always pushing the stone uphill.

Listen to that voice inside of you, your emotional being. It is giving you valuable information and energy that you need to take care of yourself all the time. You deserve to know what you are feeling, whether or not it is an appropriate feeling to act on. If you have the information, you can decide what to do with the energy that accompanies it.

Hopefully, this book has helped you find a new and different view of anger—healing energy that our body generates in response to any and every injury. What people normally think of as anger is just the aggressive, hot end of the spectrum of anger. But the cold, passive-aggressive end is just as powerful and has just as much potential energy for healing and causing damage.

I hope that you also have a better understanding about the middle range of the spectrum. These are the healthy assertive behaviors that are part of your attending to yourself and those you care about and interact with on a daily basis. These behaviors include asking others for what you need and being willing to confront conflict and misunderstandings with others, whether it is in the world of love, work, or play. Being assertive means that you know what you are feeling most of the time and are aware that you have an absolute right to feel what you feel. You'll probably find that you are drawn to others in the social and intimate worlds who recognize that you have the right to your feelings and who expect you to recognize and deal with theirs as well. Being assertive means using the information and energy that your emotions bring to you in the manner that is healthiest for each specific situation.

In addition, I hope that you now understand how anger can become dysfunctional. If it is used to distort sadness it can turn into depression. If it is confounded with fear it can create anxiety. Anger can become mixed with deprivation to lead to addictive behaviors. If it is clogged up inside of you, it can result in explosions of anger or physiological problems. These are painful, self-destructive uses of anger, but you can use this very same energy to move toward healing and fulfillment. Hopefully you now have the beginnings of a strategy to reclaim your anger for either self-nurturing or personal power.

You now know how to begin to be more in touch with yourself emotionally, to check in with yourself daily, repeatedly, to develop your emotional abilities. Journaling these feelings, as well as your personal thoughts about your growth process and the important people in your life, will help as an adjunct to therapy or to keep you on track if you're working by yourself.

The Stop, Drop, and Roll system, used to put out the fire of your dysfunctional use of anger, can help you intervene in your own problematic thoughts, feelings, and behaviors. Whether the dysfunctional anger plays out in the context of a mood problem, an anxiety problem, or addictive and compulsive behaviors, this three-step program is a guide to identify when you're on fire and how to put it out effectively. Stop, Drop, and Roll is a process and you will need to be patient with yourself as you work to:

1. Notice the problem and work to take time out and move out of the emotionally injured state.

2. Think about the problem that you've identified and put it into the perspective of your current and past emotional injuries.

3. Take some appropriate action to unbend the anger and put it to the use for which it is meant: self-nurturance and/or empowerment.

Besides understanding your own anger, I hope that you now also have some pretty solid ideas about psychotherapy and how it can work for you, as well as understand the role that anger plays in both short- and long-term treatment. In short-term work, where the focus is on dealing with here-and-now problems, you understand how those same issues may resonate with and be supported by injuries from childhood. When pursuing a full healing in treatment, you understand the dynamics of emotional injury.

These injuries are usually the result of bad parenting. Bad parenting is universal, though with vast differences in the degree from person to person, even within a single family. Bad parenting happens when anyone is parenting while in his or her own Hurt Child ego state. Since all parents are human and parent at times while they are in a place of some emotional injury, we all do some bad parenting. Bad parenting elicits the split between the "Good" Kid and the "Bad" Kid. I hope that you have learned some of the various ways this split causes dysfunction and how your anger needs to be used to both heal this split and to empower the inner child to confront and heal the Internal Bad Parents.

The information that you gain from reconnecting with your "Bad" Kid, your emotional being, is needed for you to be able to take care of yourself in relationships with other people. This is especially true in the context of emotionally intimate relationships.

Emotional intimacy is the commitment two people make to honor each other's feelings, even when they don't like those feelings. You cannot be truly emotionally intimate with someone else if you're not emotionally intimate with yourself. This means that you must acknowledge all of your important feelings, including the uncomfortable ones such as anger. In fact, you can even see anger as being a "gift" to your relationship, since you are sharing all aspects of yourself with your partner. Sharing angry feelings can allow a couple to get to the injuries that underlie the anger. Doing this emotional work with each other can lead to true love, which is the deep appreciation we deliver to each other in our attempts to cherish and keep the invisible "us" alive.

There are two differing types of conflicts in the world of emotional intimacy, real conflicts and miscommunication. All intimate conflict resolution requires fairness. Just as in the game of "Infinity Volleyball," where the only goal is to keep the ball in the air, everyone has to win or everyone is going to lose. To resolve real conflicts, the only options are compromise and/or taking turns. To resolve miscommunication conflicts, the Stop, Drop, and Roll method provides a structure for couples that are beginning to learn how to build trust and communicate with compassion, regardless of how many years they have been together.

While it's exceedingly painful to be stuck in a place of emotional darkness, it's also very easy to succumb to the pain and fear that we are exposed to every day. Whether we are in tune enough to attend to it or not, emotional injury is pervasive. We all experience it in growing up and in living each and every day. We all experience some level of abandonment in our lives. It seems much easier, at least initially, to sit back and let the damage continue. It's also easy to abandon yourself and let your anger cycle back against you in depression, anxiety, and addiction. While it's difficult to pay attention to what you are feeling and use that energy to nurture and/or empower yourself, it is the choice we must embrace because it leads to fulfillment.

Finally, please remember that all emotional injuries, on some level, are about a lack of the true love and nurturing that we all need. Usually these injuries begin in childhood. However, we also have unmet needs in our daily lives as well. Don't ever give up on working to find the real love that you need from others in this life. The energy of your anger is not meant to alienate you from others or from yourself. Your anger is not meant to isolate you and leave you feeling intimidated or hopeless. It is meant to bring you the love that you need and have been pursuing, even if you have been using your anger dysfunctionally in your recent past.

Finding the love that you need is healing for us all. Once we have been able to receive enough love to heal, fulfillment comes from returning that favor to others. I have been blessed to have made a career of giving guidance and love to others who are struggling. It is like giving sunshine, water, and fertile soil to a plant that is withering. It is miraculous to watch people take the necessary nutrients and proceed to grow and even blossom. Being able to both receive and give this energy is what fulfillment is all about. I wish this for you, and for everyone, with all of my heart.

# ACKNOWLEDGMENTS

IT SEEMS LIKE AN INTIMIDATING TASK TO MAKE SURE I acknowledge all of those who have been so helpful to me in undertaking this project. Nonetheless, I would like to start by acknowledging all of the clients with whom I have worked over the years. While accompanying them through their healing, I have grown and learned as a therapist. It is daunting to try to effectively validate their willingness to utilize the anger about their injuries, to find the courage to face their fears and commit to healing in the face of all of the difficulties that life has thrown at them.

I also need to acknowledge all of my extended and immediate family for being so supportive throughout this undertaking. This book is dedicated to my wife, Pamela, without whose support there would be no book. My children, Ariel and Jenna, have grown up listening to me talk about it, as well as watching me take time to write while we are on vacations. My oldest daughter, Ariel, has supported me intensively, with graphics for my website and presentations, as well as the cover design and the diagrams in this book. My youngest daughter, Jenna, contributed "unexpected" to the title, as well as her wonderful spirit.

My parents have contributed by the caring that they have consistently given to me throughout my life, as well as their example of a working relationship. My brother, Ned, and sister, Elka, have always been there for me. My departed sister, Isadora Jo, showed me her tenacious courage in her battles in her life. My wife's family, as well, has supplied an important, warm, and supportive family base for all of us.

I also want to thank my colleagues, who have supplied the context of discussing cases, treatment, encouragement, and plans as well as commented on my ideas. First among many is Jeff Anker, M.D. Jeff has always been a supportive friend and should probably be included in the previous paragraph, where I thanked my family.

I would like to thank the great people at Paraview. Alex Dake, the CEO, and Patrick Huyghe, editor in chief, selected my book for publication and dealt with all of my anxieties. Lisa Kaiser, my editor, was invaluable in helping me to constantly refocus my message and make this a much better book.

Also, I must mention all of the volunteer expert guests on my cable access mental health outreach television show, *Emotional Success*. All showed a willingness to share their expertise, provide information to the public, and give their precious time. I list them here, in no particular order: John Gilburt, Ph.D., Susan Hubbard, L.C.S.W., Richard Suddath, M.D., Ivan Miller, Ph.D., Gary Rosen, M.D., Gregory Steinwand, Psy.D., Dawn Taylor, Ph.D., Earle Shugerman, M.D., Patrick Vann, Ph.D., Robert Unger, Ph.D., Marilyn Coonelly, Ph.D., Mary Hartnett, Ph.D., Jim Gallagher, Psy.D., Howie Lambert, Ph.D., David Miklowitz, Ph.D., Marilla Senterfit, L.C.S.W., Bill Kipp of Model Mugging, Daniel Minerva, Ph.D., Dan Fisher, M.D., and Jonathon Woodcock, M.D. I would also like to mention Neil Rosenthal, M.A., John Gilburt, Ph.D., Burton Rosenblum, Ed.D., and Roger Cambor, M.D., who read and provided valuable critiques of my work.

Along those lines, I must thank Dona Alexis, the co-producer of my television show, *Emotional Success*, who believed in me, shared my vision, and worked so hard to make those shows a reality. Additionally, all of the technical volunteers at Boulder's cable access TV who supported those efforts have my thanks as well.

Helping me to find the path to public success, I must also thank Don Downey, of Sovereign Pictures, for his help in making my promotional video. He is truly an artist and a wonder man. Virginia Detweiler, L.C.S.W., for her support and endorsement of my book and vision deserves special thanks. Gregory Gaiser, M.A., deserves the same appreciation.

My PR person, Robin Blakely, of Livingston Communications, has been an ongoing source of inspiration, as well as my agent, Joelle Delbourgo, of Joelle Delbourgo Associates.

I would especially like to thank Evelyn Bassoff, Ph.D., Ivan Miller, Ph.D., David Miklowitz, Ph.D., Steven Dubovsky, M.D., and Jim Warner for their willingness to endorse my book.